The Stranger of Galilee

"Art thou only a stranger . . . . ?"

Luke 24:18

In fancy I stood by the shore, one day,
Of the beautiful murm'ring sea:
I saw the great crowds as they thronged the way
Of the Stranger of Galilee:
I saw how the man who was blind from birth
In a moment was made to see.
The lame was made whole by the matchless skill
Of the Stranger of Galilee:

And I felt I could love Him forever,
So gracious and tender was He,
I claimed Him that day as my Saviour,
This Stranger of Galilee.

C. H. MORRIS

Companion volume to

BENEATH THE CROSS OF JESUS
(Meditations on the Passion of Our Lord)

by the same author, who has also written

INTO THE SAME IMAGE

THEY TEACH US TO PRAY

PRAYER IS THE SECRET

The Stranger
of Galilee

Meditations on the Life of Our Lord

by

REGINALD E. O. WHITE, M.A., B.D.

Wm. B. Eerdmans Publishing Company
Grand Rapids, Michigan

Library of Congress Catalog Card Number, 60-10096

Printed in the United States of America

First edition, September 1960

For kind permission to reproduce Alice Meynell's "Christ in the Universe", grateful acknowledgement is made to the Meynell family.

CONTENTS

PREPARATIONS THAT ACCENTUATE IMPORTANCE

A time for greatness
The Advent faith
Historic roots
Rich — poor — rich
And the Child grew

1 A Time for Greatness

"The time is fulfilled . . . . "
"When the fulness of the time was come, God sent forth his Son."

Mark 1:15, Galatians 4:4

"SHOW OUR CRITICS a great man: they begin to what they call 'account' for him. He was the 'creature of the Time', they say; the Time called him forth. Alas, we have known Times call loudly enough for their great man, but not find him when they called! He was not there — Providence had not sent him. The Time, calling its loudest, had to go down to confusion and wreck because he would not come when called!"

So the vigorous Carlyle. But his fine protest against too easy explanations of greatness does not dispose of the underlying question: Does the hero owe his stature to his living in a crucial time, or is the time significant because he lived in it? Does the man make the age, or the age the man? Carlyle's own reply is that the needs and conditions of every period of history are but tinder awaiting the kindling lightning out of heaven, and "the Great Man, with his free force direct out of God's own hand, *is* the lightning".

That is well said, if we remember that God also prepared the tinder. The time, the man, and the God who brings the two together make all history's great events.

I

No age called more loudly for a Man, and for salvation, than the age in which Christ appeared. His first recorded words, as He commenced His ministry are, "The time is fulfilled . . . . " His coming is everywhere represented as the fulfilment of prophecy, the event upon which the gaze of preceding generations had been fixed, towards which a long providential ordering of history had purposefully moved. The first evangelists announced that in Him the long-awaited Day had dawned; the greatest of the apostles repeats that Christ came "in the fulness of the time".

Christ's birth thus marks man's readiness, fruit of God's agelong preparation. His death marks man's unreadiness, for there is a preparation which only man can perfect.

God made ready a time, and a people. As for the time, it is easy to point to the Roman peace, a world wide open to travel, and missionary expansion; to Roman roads designed for marching legions but equally convenient for gospel pioneers; to Roman law and social order, so often the protection of the first apostles and churches. The Empire had fused a multitude of races, welding the world into one, with a one-world ideal of culture, religion, and language. But the decay of Greek philosophy and faith had left a vacuum and hunger to which Rome had found no answer.

As for the people: by prophecy, promise, and a wondrous providence Israel was made ready to be the cradle of the Christian faith. Alone among the nations she possessed faith in one God, holy, wise, omnipotent and good; the highest known standard of ethics and of family life; and a glowing, glorious hope — the expectation of Messiah. By the time of Jesus this prepared people had spread to every centre of trade, learning, and population, and everywhere they took their vision, their hope, and two priceless treasures — their Scriptures, newly translated into a world-language, and the Synagogue — to be textbook and springboard of the gospel of Christ.

Within the Jewish faith lay two ideas awaiting clearer exposition and fulfilment. One was sacrifice. The towering Hebrew conviction of the holiness of God could be reconciled with the deeply-felt sinfulness of man only in terms of priesthood, atonement, expiation, forgiveness, sacrificial ideas familiar to Jewish minds. But not until Calvary was their inmost meaning understood.

The other imperfectly understood conception was the figure of the Servant of the Lord, foreshadowed by the later prophets. He would neither strive nor raise a clamour in the streets; He would be gentle with the bruised reed, patient with the flickering lamp. Despised, rejected of men, a man of sorrows whom the Lord Himself would bruise, He would bear man's sins, being wounded for men's transgressions that by His stripes they might be healed. Yet would He live again, see of the travail of His soul, and be content. Here, within the pages of the Jewish Bible, lay the living portrait of a wanted Saviour, the vivid likeness of Him whom the gospel declared had surely come.

This was preparation indeed. In shaping the age for the event, the people for the Man, the Lord of history and nations had done His work well. The time was fulfilled, and the world was ready.

II

But look again. That Roman peace was no gentle rule, but a military dictatorship, ruthless, and often cruel. That Roman Empire had persecuted the Jew and was soon to persecute the Christian. The decline of Greek thought had bred the grossest superstitions. A hard, inhuman cynicism possessed educated minds; a maze of Oriental mystery-cults with secret, often obscene rites and morbid, sometimes vicious doctrines fascinated the multitude. Great Roman cities were dens of vice and cruelty. Roman pomp and luxury were raised on slavery and plunder.

Paul's picture of the moral rottenness of pagan society, sketched in his letter to the Romans, is amply confirmed by the satirists of the imperial period, and his hint in Thessalonians of strong forces of disruption working beneath the surface of Roman order was equally well founded. One of the greatest of classical historians declares: "The world was growing old, and not even Caesar could make it young again".

> *And o'er the heathen world disgust*
> *And secret loathing fell,*
> *Deep weariness, and sated lust,*
> *Made human life a hell.*

Men everywhere were calling it a godless time, a god-forsaken age. Yet God prepared it.

And even Israel's faith burned low. Strict Judaism was frequently a hollow and unlovely thing; Pharisee and scribe were alienated from the common Jews as from the Gentiles. Many besides the Sadducees were eager for worldly compromise with Rome and a profitable exploitation of the pagan. Paul charges Jews with theft, adultery, sacrilege, dishonouring the law, so that through them "the very name of God is blasphemed among the Gentiles". The rise of numerous reforming sects, and some contemporary Jewish literature, again confirm his verdict.

In the ghettos of Alexandria, Corinth, Rome, and Ephesus the Jew was far below his best; his name was frequently a byword, his ways despised, his pride resented bitterly. And had not Jesus spoken, with tears in His far-seeing eyes, of coming days when Judah's house would be left unto her desolate?

So God prepared a time, and it seemed a godless time. God prepared a people, and they seemed a faithless people. Yet at that time and through that people God did the unimaginable thing.

III

It is ever so. That was a day of upheaval and restlessness, of the movement of peoples and the clash of cultures, of the shaking of established ideas of religion and life, when Abraham walked out of Ur of the Chaldees to seek a land and a faith on which the future would be built. The powerful Church of the West rose phoenix-like from the bloodshed and agony, ruin and flame of the dying Roman world.

Luther, standing at the rebirth of Europe and the reformation of the Church could declare: "This age is Satan's own". John Richard Green says of England two hundred years ago: "Never had religion seemed at a lower ebb; the Church had sunk to insignificance, the bulk of the clergy were indolent, lax and poor; statesmen are unbelievers and grossly immoral; purity and fidelity are sneered out of fashion; twenty young thieves are hung in one day in one prison . . . . " Who could have guessed that in that age God was preparing the Wesleys and Whitefield for England, the Haldanes for Scotland, and Carey for the world?

So in the greatest time of all God turned to a peasant home at Nazareth — and we know what men thought of Nazareth; to a carpenter's family without wealth, name, rank or influence. The Babe's first visitors were shepherds, whom rabbis despised as "next door to heathen". His followers were gathered from outcasts and sinners, His Church composed of not many wise or mighty, noble or known, led by "unlearned and ignorant men".

Always the time made ready remains to our eyes unpropitious, the people prepared seem to human judgement still unpromising. God's preparation is hidden in man's unpreparedness, and the surest sign that God is at work is ardent response beset by equally ardent opposition.

IV

That is why the armorial crest of the Greatest of all time's heroes contains both swaddling clothes and a manger. These are the very credentials of the Christ: "this shall be a sign unto you, ye shall find the babe wrapped in swaddling clothes, lying in a manger". What sign is this? For many a babe a mother's excited fingers had prepared the linen winding sheets in loving anticipation; many and many an infant had been driven forth, by poverty or shame, to spend his first night in a manger.

The sign lies in the two together, the preparation and the unpreparedness. The swaddling clothes enshrine the eager welcome of Mary, and of pious Israel; the shut door of the hostelry prefigures His rejection by a world too self-absorbed to let its Saviour in. The time had called for Him, and did not want Him. He was long awaited and soon rejected, passionately desired and passionately hated, loved and crucified. Therein lies the clearest index to His Saviourhood.

God had done much to make straight His way, but the doors of human hearts only human hands can open. Therein lies a solemn warning. But hope too: for the God who in unpropitious times and through unpromising people redeems mankind, bids us despair of no age and of no generation while His day of grace shall last.

2 *The Advent Faith*

"The Lord, whom ye seek, shall suddenly come."
"The dayspring from on high hath visited us."
" . . . This, the time of thy visitation."

Malachi 3:1, Luke 1:78, 19:44

"Is NOT GOD in the height of the heaven? Well, behold the height of the stars, how high they are! And thou sayest, How doth God know? can he judge through the dark cloud? . . . What *can* the Almighty do . . . ?" Eliphaz the Temanite, arguing with Job, expresses unwittingly the deepest complaint of paganism, the cry of the suffering against the heartless indifference of heaven. One Psalmist asks, in doubt, "How doth God know? Is there knowledge in the most High?" and another answers with despair: "God hath forgotten, he hideth his face". A patriarch cries in anguish, "Oh that I knew where I might find him!", and a prophet replies, "Verily thou art a God that hidest thyself!"

The complaint lingers. Tennyson's Lotos-eaters vow to

> *lie reclined*
> *On the hills like gods together, careless of mankind*

and Shakespeare makes Gloucester declare:

> *As flies to wanton boys are we to th' gods;*
> *They kill us for their sport*

while Fitzgerald turns scepticism to scorn —

> *. . . that inverted Bowl we call The Sky,*
> *Whereunder crawling coop't we live and die,*
> *Lift not thy hands to It for help — for It*
> *Rolls impotently on as Thou or I.*

So deep runs the doubt, rising at times to an accusing fear, that God does not care; that heaven is deaf and blind, remote, aloof; that the universe is at heart without compassion.

Far different is the Bible's central emphasis. From the first poetic pictures of God walking with Adam in the cool of the garden to the final vision of the New Jerusalem descending out of heaven that God might dwell with men,

16

the underlying message of Biblical religion is of a God who Himself comes forth to meet with men, and who complains of *man's* aloofness — "ye would not".

I

The essential and timeless truth beneath the whole Advent-to-Easter story is found, with varying degrees of clarity but with unchanging certainty, on every page of Scripture: God has made Himself known, has taken action in history. The Lord of Hosts has invaded our beaches, and established a bridgehead within our world of time and space, events and people. The God who seemed aloof has intervened.

Throughout the history of Israel, from Abraham and Moses to the prophets and the Exile, men saw the hand of God at work, the heart of God laid bare. Throughout, He is the God whose Word has come to men; and on the last page of the Old Testament that Word finds final and perfect expression in the promise, "The Lord, whom ye seek, shall suddenly come".

Nor is the expectation disappointed. The New Testament opens with news of the divine inbreaking in the coming of a Child. A prophet appears proclaiming the divine King's imminent arrival. Jesus declares that the finger of God is stirring that generation. His entry to Jerusalem is her day of God's own visitation.

Easter brings the crowning point of God's unanswerable intervention into man's experience. At Pentecost once more the divine invades the human. On the Damascus road, God steps unheralded into Paul's life-story, and the apostolic Church lives in the constant and exciting expectation of an ultimate and final intervention that shall mark the end of the age.

From first to last the New Testament is saturated with this "Advent" faith, this confident assurance and compelling hope of God's continually doing new things. The first Christians lived in this atmosphere of Advent, expecting God to intervene savingly into every situation. God was all about them, and *anything* could happen.

Unlike the gods who lie beside their nectar, careless of mankind, the God of the Bible has stepped forth, and stepped down. He has entered history, has lain within a manger, and walked with men.

II

The New Testament presentation of this Advent truth is no mere repetition of the Old: the differences are striking. In Old Testament stories of God's invasion of human life the setting is often awesome and terrifying. In clouds and earthquake, smoke and flame, God came at Sinai. In flaming fire and rolling chariot of indescribable glory He showed Himself to Ezekiel. Storm, judgement, and the melting of the mountain-tops are in Isaiah's description. The heavens are rent, the earth is shaken before the majesty of God, the demonstration of might, the threat of judgement.

Contrast this vivid imagery and its implications with the Bethlehem story. Here God's intervention wears a very different aspect. He comes in an act of surpassing spiritual splendour, amid joy and singing. All that is tenderest, holiest, loveliest in human relationships — home, motherhood, infancy, the simplicities and the strength of love's noblest loyalties — is made the setting of the Advent. Wise men bring their treasures in token of the far world's homage. The successors of the best known of all Bethlehem's shepherds welcome David's greater son. The songs of the mother and her kinswoman are echoed by angelic choirs that sing God's glory and man's peace in the night skies — and God is here!

G. K. Chesterton's moving description of the coming of St. Francis into the darkness and gloom of the Middle Ages applies with equal truth to the coming of the Christ: "It was the end of a long stern night . . . . He stood with his hands uplifted, about him was a burst of birds singing, and behind him was the break of day".

Christ, too, had been heralded as the Dayspring from on high, the Sun of righteousness arising with healing in His beams, and the lyrics of St. Luke are but the dawn chorus of the world's most glorious springtime.

So, in place of the elemental violence of earthquake, fire, and storm the vehicle of the divine Advent is now seen to be — a human personality. The Word was made *flesh,* and like unto His brethren. We beheld glory, still, but it was enshrined in the lowliness and frailty of a human frame, and expressed through the limitations of a human nature. In place of some stupendous spectacle in the skies, God enters history through the channel of a human life. Earthquake, wind, and fire may show the greatness of His might: it takes a human heart to manifest the glory full of grace and truth.

Yet more startling is the third contrast with Old Testament descriptions. There God comes with irresistible power, bearing down all opposition by divine omnipotence. In the Advent story, the arch-villain's shadow, with the shape of Herod, falls at once across the cradle. The Child is from the first rejected from the inn, and flees a refugee to Egypt. Angelic hosts, "winged squadrons of the sky", the twelve legions that stood ready in Gethsemane for the call that never came, keep ceaseless watch above the sleeping village. Herod and Caiaphas, Pilate and Caesar lie in wait for Him, and He will keep tryst with angels once again — within a tomb.

The Captain of our salvation enters personally within our conflict. He bears our griefs and carries our sorrows; He tastes death for every man. The Advent message is not all merry sentiment divorced from life's realities: the manger is the first step towards the cross. Already a sword pierces Mary's heart, myrrh is among His birthday gifts, He is a sign that shall be spoken against, and weeping is heard in Ramah. For the Son of Man came to give His life. He was born to die; not to bear down opposition with superior might but to win acceptance through suffering and death.

III

These characteristic features of God's coming amongst men are significant, illuminating, saving. But the essential truth lies not in the form, merely, but in the fact of God's invasion. Jesus is God's flat denial of any impassable gulf between Himself and man.

And the truth is not limited to Christ's life and death, or to some far-off age and place. We, too, can live in the atmosphere of Advent, for God is always intervening, constantly breaking into our experience — if we will.

Far too easily we assume a *horizontal* view of Christian faith. We believe that God did something long ago, and ever since the ripples of that great event have spread outwards, levelling through history, reaching across the centuries to touch our lives and wash on past us to the rising generations. That is true. But there is a *vertical* perspective too. God breaks into every age, in every generation, into every life that opens up to Him. The spreading ripples on the pool of history are spattered all the time with the divine rain of inbreaking power and love and grace doing new and refreshing things in each new time.

For the Advent truth is timeless: there is a perpetual coming, a ceaseless intervention of the divine. That is the meaning of the doctrine of the Spirit, and until we appreciate its glorious possibilities we live impoverished lives, too easily exhausted, too soon cast down. As Jesus said to Nicodemus, the experience of the Kingdom always begins with the inbreaking of new life from above. Salvation comes, not by the rearrangement of human motives and resources, but through the invasion of a divine initiative with superhuman energies.

There lies the Christian hope for old men (like Nicodemus), for old churches, for an aging world. God stands not aloof: He still breaks in. We celebrate each Christmas the perpetual invasion of the liberating forces of the Advent Christ!

3 Historic Roots

"The Word became flesh, and dwelt among us."
"Now once in the end of the age hath he appeared."
"Where Christ should be born . . . . In Bethlehem of Judaea."
John 1:14, Hebrews 9:26, Matthew 2:4-5

THE CONSISTENT TESTIMONY of Scripture and of Christian experience tells of the constant incoming of God, with gracious purpose and with saving effect, into every willing life. But the coming of Jesus is more than a symbol for a timeless religious truth. His advent was neither timeless, constant, nor repeated, but fixed, and once for all. It belongs to one epoch, one place, one particular time-sequence in the story of the race. Possessing a universal, timeless significance, it is no less marked by a particular, temporal reality. The advent is not merely a truth, but a fact. It happened.

I

Luke's sixfold date sets Jesus' story firmly within His age and the context of history. It all happened, he says, during Rome's supremacy, under Pilate's governorship, while Herod ruled. Matthew fixes the time no less definitely as the end of an age, the fulfilment of a period of prophecy and promise. Tacitus, Suetonius, Pliny, Josephus are "profane" historians who pass their comment upon the appearance of Jesus as part of the secular history of mankind. And the emphasis upon historic certainty can be spiritually important.

Then, as now, there were those who looked anywhere but in their own time for evidence of God's activity. Traditionalists looked backwards, to Moses, and David, and the prophets. Apocalyptists, with their dreams of divine denouement in the golden future, gazed ever forwards. Others again looked for no "actual" timely sign of God's redeeming power, but reduced all spiritual truth to abstract principles, remote from daily life. For all three types of mind, faith represents a never-never hope that God does things somehow, sometime, any other time but *now*.

Against such vague, disembodied, abstract religiousness stands Luke's firm insistence upon the historic act of God. The time is fulfilled, the Kingdom is at hand. Christ belongs not to eternity alone, but now and always to time and to the present. He confronts each age. "Today, if ye will hear His voice, harden not your hearts . . . ."

II

Matthew takes equal pains to fix the place to which Christ came: Bethlehem Ephratah, Judah, and again Bethlehem. We talk much, and truly, about the universal Christ, available everywhere: it is easy sometimes to suppose that that means nowhere in particular. Jesus Himself warns against the temptation to think that God is somewhere else than where we are; when men say, Lo here, or there, it is not so: the Kingdom is among you, here and now!

"Who shall ascend into heaven," asks Paul, "to bring Christ down from above? or who shall descend into the deep to bring Christ up from the dead?" Or who shall travel across the seas to mission-lands of great revival to bring Christ home from abroad? His Kingdom is not *from* the world, as originating out of it; but neither is it a Kingdom "out of this world" — it is very much in it. On earth the Kingdom is to come, the Father's will be done. The Christian life is to be lived, not merely waited for, or dreamed about.

For Jesus came into the *here*, as He came into the *now*, of daily life, and here and now He is to be accepted, served, and followed.

III

As Luke emphasises the particular time, and Matthew the particular place, of Jesus' coming, so John lays stress upon the form: "the Word became flesh". Christ came the way of real humanity, and dwelt among us. Weary and thirsty, He rested by a well; He prayed as we pray, He asked questions, He exulted in spirit, and again He groaned, weeping beside the grave of one He loved, carrying our sorrows. He understood our nature from within, craved human fellowship, resisted temptation, experienced pain, and tasted death.

It is truly astonishing how, with so much to tell of the self-revelation of the divine Son, John still insists at every point upon the humanity of Christ. He came from God, and went to God: but He lived out in time, in this world, and in our nature, His perfect life of love.

Certainly we have to keep in mind, in our distant twentieth century, that Christ is timeless, universal Lord, belonging to all generations, lands, and worlds. But Advent rightly reminds us that He came at a particular point in history, to a particular location on the map, in the particular form of human nature, to this real and perplexing and demanding world we know. Here He chose to belong. And here we are called to be His, and to build His Kingdom. The Christian must not try to become more "spiritual" — more otherworldly — than his Lord!

IV

But the point has more than practical significance. It is intellectually wise to remember that our faith was born in Bethlehem, in the gospel of the manger and the star. It is mentally bracing to recall that our whole conviction and experience stand not in theories, philosophies, or aspirations, but in unalterable, historic acts of God.

The gospel, that is to say, is not just one way of thinking which some other newer, cleverer way of thinking may one day "disprove", or even replace. The fact of Christ, the quality of His life, the impact of His words and deeds upon mankind, are written unalterably into the past for believer and unbeliever, agnostic and scoffer, alike; and for all future time.

Of course, the historic events carry a whole train of meanings and consequences in Christian experience: but it is not the explanation or the experience which are our foundation, but the facts. If the Christian interpretation of what happened is not the true one, that does not dispose entirely of the story. Some other, more adequate interpretation must be found. And "more adequate" means accounting better for the story, for the influence of Jesus upon history, for the endless good that has flowed from Christian inspiration, for the daily experience of millions who find in Christ their Saviour, Friend, and Lord and who, living by His standards and His grace, live well.

Whatever men say, there in history stands the Christ, His voice echoing down the centuries, His peerless life still unassailed, the torch of His truth still throwing its revealing light upon our lives. Feelings may fluctuate, times may change, but our faith is rooted in the unalterable historic event that began in a manger and ended — insofar as it has ever ended — with an empty tomb.

V

Moreover, this thing that happened is something that *God* did. As our faith rests on no merely human thinking, so it is not the result of any merely human action or endeavour. The Christian life, with all its heights and depths of faith and effort, of prayer and consecration, of character and service, is in the end just our response of gratitude and love to what God did for us before we knew of it, or could possibly deserve it.

Sometimes we forget this, too, and Christian endurance becomes exacting, Christian service drudgery. Duty replaces delight, and obligation takes the place of gladness. We become intent again on trying to save ourselves, to deserve God's blessing. Then it is a renewal of peace, a recapturing of joy, to remember that it all began with God's doing for our sake what we could never do for ourselves. Jesus is God's *gift* to a sinful world: all God asks is that we accept His Son.

This is our faith: that God has broken into human history, in an unalterable event, on His own gracious initiative, with supreme beauty and in saving power. Time, place, and manner are precisely fixed; the significance and efficacy of what He did we know within our hearts. This is the gospel of the nativity — a sure faith, steadfastly fixed on strong foundations and calling for a glad thanksgiving and a grateful life. The Son of God has come: thanks be unto God for His unspeakable gift.

4 Rich – Poor – Rich

"Ye know the grace of our Lord Jesus Christ, that, though he was rich, yet for your sakes he became poor, that ye through his poverty might be rich."

II Corinthians 8:9

AN AMAZING VARIETY of metaphors is used in the New Testament to state the essential Advent fact. Christ's coming is the dawn of a new era, the measure of divine love, the final step in an agelong redemptive process, the last word in divine revelation, God's answer to the working of the devil, the conveyance of life eternal, and an example to be emulated. But most surprising of all, it is an argument for financial generosity.

Urging a charitable gesture of sympathy by the Gentile churches towards the poorer Christians at Jerusalem faced with famine conditions and famine prices, Paul suddenly sees the whole mission of Christ in just these terms of poverty and wealth, of need and enrichment, of man's insolvency and God's bountiful gift. "Ye know the generosity of the Lord Jesus, how that though he was rich, yet for your sakes he became poor, that ye through his poverty might be rich". Could any Christian Gentile heart resist an argument so cogent, appealing to divine example, glorious experience, and simple gratitude all at once?

I

He was rich, Paul declares, unveiling in a phrase the inexhaustible sufficiency out of which resources for salvation were ultimately drawn.

We shall not get far with attempts to define that eternal richness of the pre-existent Christ. Scripture must suffice. Jesus declared, "I am the living bread which came down from heaven"; asked His accusers, "What if you were to see the Son of man ascending where he was before?"; and prayed with His disciples, "Father, glorify thou me with the glory which I had with thee before the world was". John comments: "In the beginning was the Word, and the Word was with God, and the Word was God . . . . And the Word became flesh". Paul himself elaborates the statement "He was rich" in memorable fashion: "Being in the form of God, he did not think of equality with God as a thing to be held on to at all costs, but emptied himself". Varying the terms, but not the meaning, the Epistle to the Hebrews says, "He was the outshining of the Father's glory and the express image of his person". "Thou art the Christ, the Son of the living God" is Peter's amazed confession.

Such statements baffle imagination and defy precise analysis. Equality and co-eternity with God are certainly implied. Certainly also an absolute identity of purpose and will between the Father and the Son is affirmed: "God so loved . . . that he gave his only begotten Son . . . spared not his own Son . . . . The Father sent the Son to be the Saviour of the world". These are statements echoed readily in Jesus' heart: "I do always those things which please him . . . . My meat is to do the will of him that sent me . . . . This commandment have I received of my Father".

But the "richness" of the pre-existing Christ has far-reaching implications for Christian experience as well as for Christian thought. For the Scripture's affirmations imply in Christ's divinity a glory, a fulness, a limitless wealth of grace and power *available* for the task Christ came to do. Upon the divinity of the eternal Son is based the sufficiency of Christ to save. "In him dwelleth all the fulness of the Godhead bodily" declares the Christian theologian; and "of his fulness have all we received" answers the Christian saint. "It pleased the Father that in him should all fulness dwell" argues the apostle in the full flight of speculative thought: "and ye are complete in him" he adds, returning at once to his pastoral concern for those who read.

Thus what appears to be remote theology, a theory of scholars, a shibboleth of orthodoxy, is in fact the qualification of Jesus for His colossal task. The will to save is not enough if power and authority be wanting. Our poor world has more than enough of poverty-stricken saviours! Christ was rich, and consequently able and sufficient to save.

II

He became poor, and came to Bethlehem, accepting the limitations of a human life. The divine Son condescended to share our weakness of body and weariness of spirit; He lived by faith, and knew the anguish of the prayer that could not be granted. He faced loneliness, homelessness that left Him with nowhere to lay His head, the bitterness of betrayal. Criticism, abuse, slander, ingratitude, injustice, and physical violence bore hard upon His sensitive soul. Men unworthy of the power they wielded used it shamefully against Him, and at last with cruel brutalities they took His life. He had become, willingly, very poor indeed.

The seven steps of this grievous self-impoverishment are analysed by Paul. "Being in the form of God, he [1] thought equality with God not to be grasped after, but [2] emptied himself and [3] took upon him the form of a servant, and [4] was made in the likeness of men; and being found in fashion as a man [5] he humbled himself, and [6] became obedient unto death, even [7] the death of the cross". In Milton's moving words,

> *That glorious Form, that Light unsufferable,*
> *And that far-beaming blaze of Majesty,*
> *Wherewith He wont at Heaven's high council-table*
> *To sit the midst of Trinal Unity,*
> *He laid aside; and here with us to be*
>   *Forsook the courts of everlasting day,*
>   *And chose with us a darksome house of mortal clay.*

It is tempting to dilute the truth with shallow notions of a pretended emptying and a mock humanity: but the great Bible words must stand — He emptied Himself, was made in the likeness of men, took the form of a servant; He was made a little lower than the angels, made flesh, made like unto His brethren, made of the seed of David; He partook of flesh and blood — the Man, Christ Jesus — He became poor. This is self-abnegation deliberate, gracious, ruthlessly self-imposed, the process and the price of Saviourhood. To the needed resources is wedded the necessary identification with men: redeeming humanity from within humanity, He is perfectly able to save because He perfectly understands the souls He seeks.

III

That ye through his poverty might be rich — and this, of course, is the new note, the stimulating, unexpected idea. Yet is it everywhere in the New Testament: "He hath filled the hungry with good things . . . . We have treasure in earthen vessels . . . . We preach the unsearchable riches of Christ . . . the riches of the glory of his inheritance in the saints . . . . The poor in this world, rich in faith . . . itself gold tried in the crucible; having nothing, we possess all things".

Was it because some, like Barnabas, had brought into the common coffers of the Church all that they possessed, that this thought of enrichment in Christ was precious to Christian minds? Was it because so many, like Paul, had forfeited family and inheritance by choosing Christ? Was it because so many were slaves, the dispossessed of the Roman world, dreaming of pearly gates and golden streets, music, wealth, and feasting as the negro slaves sang of shoes and robe, of chariots and freedom?

Or was it just because Jesus had spoken much of the true riches, the treasure laid up in heaven secure from moth and rust and thieves, or hid in a field for the finding, offered in the market for the purchasing? Had He not promised that there was no one who had left houses or family or lands for His sake and the gospel's who would not receive a hundredfold "now in this time", and in the world to come life everlasting?

Whatever the reason, or the source of their language, first-century Christians were joyfully aware of the enrichment of life that Christ had brought them. "All things are yours," Paul could tell the poorer Corinthians, "and ye are Christ's, and Christ is God's".

> *How vast the treasure we possess!*
> *How rich Thy bounty, King of grace!*
> *This world is ours, and worlds to come;*
> *Earth is our lodge, and heaven our home:*
> *All things are ours. . . .*

Nor was the meaning of such language vague: riches of understanding and knowledge, insight and truth for impoverished minds and shallow hearts; unsearchable riches of grace and favour, blessing and peace for starved, penurious souls; riches in glory for empty lives with nothing to anticipate but a bankrupt future. God had given in Christ "all things that pertain unto life and godliness", so that the man of God was "thoroughly furnished unto every good work".

In prosperous days, when welfare legislation and boom-time economics have taken the sting from poverty and lessened the fears of insecurity, the language of poverty and riches, of the spiritual wealth to be found in Christ, loses much of its force. Yet to know on what low margins of resources some people live, of the beggarly mental and spiritual turnover by which the business of some souls is precariously conducted, makes one pause.

"Thou sayest I am rich, and increased with goods, and have need of nothing; and knowest not that thou art wretched, and miserable, and poor, and blind, and naked" might be spoken to modern Babylon as to ancient Laodicea. And the invitation still stands: "I counsel thee to buy of me gold tried in the fire, that thou mayest be rich".

Out of His eternal richness, Christ embraced immeasurable poverty, that we through His impoverishment might know unending wealth. Ye know the grace of the Lord Jesus — does He know your gratitude?

5 And the Child Grew

"And the child grew, and waxed strong in spirit, filled with wisdom: and the grace of God was upon him . . . . And Jesus increased in wisdom and stature, and in favour with God and man."   Luke 2:40, 52

PUBLICITY is the life-blood of present-day success. If the world at large is not chattering our names, the billboards blazing abroad our virtues, crowds flocking to witness our achievements, we think we have failed. Yet of the greatest life-story in the history of mankind, ten-elevenths were spent in nearly complete obscurity, mostly unrecorded, almost unknown. So silently is real greatness fashioned. So quietly does God prepare His men.

I

Jesus came to Nazareth from Egypt, a returning refugee. Inhuman tyranny then as now drove men from home and fatherland to seek shelter in strange places: like the inn in His babyhood, and the city in His manhood, so now in His boyhood the land of God's choice expelled for a time the Chosen of God.

At Nazareth He grew in wisdom as in stature, and in favour with God and man. Across the nearby hills, camel-trains bore merchandise from distant lands, reminding Him of the "kingdoms of this world and all the glory of them". The signs of Roman rule were everywhere, strutting soldiers, overbearing commanders, rules of occupation, ubiquitous tax-collectors, to impress young Jewish minds with the foreigner's supremacy. Young men of Nazareth could be conscripted to travel a mile as unpaid attendants under martial law, as Jesus knew. Was He ever so compelled?

Against this wider background Jesus read, with lively imagination, of the great battles that ravaged Galilee when Syria, Assyria, Egypt, and then Greece had fought upon Esdraelon, and Samaria had been the fortress of the north. His was no dream world untouched by hatred, violence, and war.

30

Yet Nazareth itself was unpretentious. Among her quiet slopes He learned

> *To look on nature, not as in the hour*
> *Of thoughtless youth; but hearing oftentimes*
> *The still, sad music of humanity,*

and felt the Presence that disturbs with joy of elevated thoughts,

> *a sense sublime*
> *Of something far more deeply interfused,*
> *Whose dwelling is the light of setting suns,*
> *And the round ocean and the living air,*
> *And the blue sky, and in the mind of man;*
> *A motion and a spirit, that impels*
> *All thinking things, all objects of all thought,*
> *And rolls through all things.*

But He was no recluse. Charming echoes of children's games in Nazareth's market place, pretended weddings and funerals, and the picture of a sulky child who would not play, provide apt illustrations later on. Did He ever act the bridegroom — or the dead?

Life in that peasant's home could not be easy. The cheapest possible sacrifices for His infant Presentation tell their tale, and artlessly His manhood's words reveal the boyhood memories. The cheapest food is five sparrows for two farthings; hungry children plead for bread, and eggs, and fish! and though a father cannot give all they ask, he will not mock with stones and scorpions. The best patch is one of cloth as old as the garment, lest the first laundering rend it: where did Jesus learn that housewifely lore? — or the recipe for bread: one handful of leaven in three measures of meal and give it time to rise!

The cheapest ovens place the fuel inside, He knows, and women will talk while grinding at the mill. He remembers the consternation caused by sudden guests, the rush through the darkened village to a neighbour's house for food. He can tell of fewer candles in advantageous places for economy, and recalls the haggling over prices in the market place, the awful language youngsters overheard.

Jesus remembers, too, the serious loss of hoarded clothing and utensils due to moth and rust, or worse, to burglary. He enters feelingly into the desolating loss of a coin from the bridal headdress heirloom, the feverish spring cleaning, the unrestrained joy at its recovery. He knows the value of the missing sheep to a shepherd who must replace it or accept dismissal. Somewhere, sometime, He learned the anguish of a home bereft of a wayward, wicked son. He was Himself an elder brother.

At least seven children made the family. There surely began His matchless skill in telling stories, and perhaps His memory of sons who could say "Yes, Father" and not do the task appointed. If we could be certain that Jude of the epistle was Christ's younger brother, what delightful memories of walks on Galilean hills would gather round the beautiful benediction: "Now unto him who is able to keep you from falling, and to present you faultless before his Father's presence with exceeding joy, be glory . . . ".

Mark reveals that Jesus was known as son of *Mary,* and this together with the silence about Joseph and Christ's consigning Mary to John's care at the end, supports the view that Mary was now widowed. Jesus is Himself "the carpenter" — "my easy yoke" is reminiscent of His acquired skill. Later the village is astonished at His learning, as though His education had been interrupted. Here is the explanation, homely but significant, of His waiting so long before beginning His work. Duties must be fulfilled in order of precedence. First the mother and family must be cared for, in obedience to the sacred law: until oncoming younger ones can release the Christ for ministry and death.

Who can imagine what tenderness her eldest son brought to Mary in her widowhood? Long afterward He felt a special care for those defenceless and alone before the rapacity of evil men. How He flayed the scribe's readiness to take advantage of the widow, urgently needing money to bury her dead, mortgaging her home on terms she could not read, and finding herself homeless before the year was out! With what quick eye and ready praise He singled out the widow's gift at the Temple treasury — "all she had". Again, with what scathing words He describes the conscienceless judge beset by the importunate entreaties of a widow seeking justice. Did not memory barb such words, and quicken His compassion for the widow of Nain, now bereaved also of her only son?

It is shameful for one to despise the home from which he

came, to affect to owe nothing to the love that bore him. The common things of simple life and domestic duty, poverty, toil, motherhood, infancy, home and family relationship are all transfigured because He lived at Nazareth and laboured. It remains an essential part of Christlikeness, as the Gospels represent it, to be an obedient son, a loving brother, a faithful workman, a sharer of burdens and defender of the right in near and homely things. For there, at Nazareth, Jesus began to expound His law and show forth His glory — in the perfection of a wholesome manliness.

II

Of the inner life and growth of the hidden years, reverence must speak less confidently. Attempts of apocryphal writers to read back into childhood the authority and power of later years are repulsive, self-refuting. Jesus was no infant prodigy. Regular attendance at school and synagogue "as his custom was" He shared with every Jewish boy; His acute knowledge of the Scriptures, and acceptance of the simple piety and prayerfulness of that village home are beyond doubt.

At twelve He became a "son of the law", and a visit to Jerusalem brought Him for the first time within the Temple. All the wonder and curiosity of childhood are stamped upon Luke's moving story; so is His parents' implicit trust in His obedience. The fruits of His religious training are seen in His haunting of the sacred precincts, His understanding of the Scriptures, His eagerness to learn — though His questioning of the doctors is disastrously misunderstood when He is represented as putting them through their paces! Most significant of all is His already maturing sense of being "a dedicated spirit", necessarily engaged "about his Father's affairs".

Heaven lay about Him in His infancy. But whereas of others it is written

> Shades of the prison house begin to close
>   Upon the growing boy,
> But he beholds the light, and whence it flows,
>   He sees it in his joy;
> The youth, who daily farther from the east
>   Must travel, still is nature's priest,

And by the vision splendid
Is on his way attended;
At length the man perceives it die away,
And fade into the light of common day,

of Him it is recorded: "He grew in favour with God". The deep insights later revealed in His free exposition of the sacred texts tell their own story of His opening mind, diligent study, and penetrating thought. A fully developed assurance of His special relation to the heavenly Father is stamped upon every word and action with which His ministry opens. So when the call of John to prepare for the imminent messianic Kingdom sounded from the Jordan valley through the towns of Galilee, it found the soul of Jesus uniquely prepared to respond, one step at a time, and with the first step — His baptism — to reach the end of preparation and the beginning of His work.

A godly home, religious institutions, sacred learning, appreciation of nature, training in prayer, a heart uniquely sensitive to every divine approach — these are the influences that fashioned the soul of the incarnate Christ to be the perfect instrument in God's hands for the redemption of the world.

III

Christ came and grew among the common things of life, the Christ of home, of childhood, of seashore and market place, of synagogue and workbench and grave. And we must keep Him there. It is fatally easy, amid the traditions, the creeds and rituals, elaborate or simple, of conventional Christianity, to lose sight altogether of the Man, Christ Jesus. It is possible to be so concerned for the truth of His divinity as to miss the glory of His humanity, pattern of our childhood, youth, and manhood. Yet must we follow His Nazareth steps if we would follow all the way, and be prepared, like Him, for wider tasks by fulfilling every call of God that finds us nearer home.

BEGINNINGS THAT DEFINE INTENTION

Wilderness campaign
Revelations at the riverside
Paths to a throne
Nazareth manifesto
Recruiting colleagues

6 Wilderness Campaign

"John came, neither eating nor drinking . . . . More than a prophet. For this is he of whom it is written, Behold, I send my messenger before thy face, which shall prepare thy way before thee."   Matthew 11:18, 9-10

It was a curious place for a campaign of any kind, on the very edge of a wilderness. Not far away lay populous Jerusalem with its paved streets, open Temple courtyard, religious atmosphere: but the prophet John would have none of these. To the north lay Galilee's numerous markets, quiet hillsides, crowded shores and townships, but John would not seek people out. Deliberately choosing desert places, he let the crowds come out to him. And they did.

I

The deepest reason for choosing this unattractive setting for prophetic ministry derives from ancient Hebrew history. Always in the background of Hebrew religion there lingered tribal memories of austere nomadic ancestors roaming scattered pastures with their flocks, and stories of the wilderness wandering of Israel under the greatest of all her men of God. Prophet after prophet had denounced the luxury, the avarice, the commercialism and license of the new-fangled cities, recalling Israel to her oldest tradition of the open places and the lonely hills, where men listened to God's voice, did justly, loved mercy, and walked humbly with their God.

So Elijah had come from desert places to challenge the loose-living court of Ahab. So Amos had come from his herdsman's vigils under the Pleiades on the open tops of the Judean hills. And so John came, no polished city dandy with high-pressure religious salesmanship to woo the multitude, but stern, puritan, full of warning. Brusque manner, rough clothing, uncultured ways, harsh language, stern message, all are in prophetic character. This, John would say, is God's Word. Take it or leave it. But you had better take it.

Many a man has been called to minister in a wilderness; to do hard things in hard days among an unresponsive people. Nowadays we should scarcely consider such a man "successful", and some would wonder if he were a man of God! There is, however, more to be learned here than faithfulness to unrewarding tasks. There is the lesson, ever hardest to accept when the wind is contrary, that truth is more important, and more imperative, than popularity.

Prophets of a smooth gospel, crying peace and safety and assurance in evil days, wooing the crowds by easily asserted platitudes and generalities, betray their calling, their God, and in the end their hearers. In an age of moral drift and mental fog, of hedonist ethics and uninhibited self-seeking, any genuine recall to religion has got to sound from the deserts of austerity in the language of moral discipline. Unless the wicked forsake his way, he cannot return to a holy God.

And it might be that such a strong approach to the problem of evangelism would prove to be good policy as well as sound theology. An observer as acute as T. S. Eliot has said that in our time discipline of the emotions is even rarer than discipline of the mind, and comments, "You will never attract the young by making Christianity easy: but a good many can be attracted by finding it difficult — difficult both to the disorderly mind and to the unruly passions". In the great crises of life most men prefer the truth, and the blunt invitation to "blood and toil and tears and sweat" evoked more loyalty and effort than all the glowing promises of ease and plenty that eloquence could devise. For serious minds a desert campaign has real attractions!

II

John's message was closely in harmony with his appearance and his background. He came as herald of the King; the way of the Lord was to be made plain, rough places smooth, crooked roads straight, for the coming of the Christ. Hearts now wayward must become the highway of the Lord. Men must think again about their lives, and change their ways. All must *repent*.

Contradicting all the Jewish pride of race, of heritage, of divine election, John declared there could be no messianic

Kingdom, no acceptance by the King, without repentance and remission. There could be no divine enthronement without dethronement of selfishness and sin. He demanded a *religious* revolution.

John left no doubt what that would mean. For the wealthy it involved the sharing out of life's good things. For soldiers in occupied territory, the renunciation of all ill-treatment of civilians, of violence and plunder, false accusation, blackmail. It meant for the discontented and the avaricious a purified and temperate ambition; it involved for civil servants empowered to extort taxes a new code of honesty and fair treatment. From all, the prophet demanded that repentance should be registered in symbolic public washing in the Jordan — a baptism of penitence leading to forgiveness.

If men refused, John offered no hope. Either a baptism of water, or else a baptism of fire. Men would be cleansed, Israel would be purified, either by penitence or judgement, by forgiveness or disaster.

And this searching, forbidding announcement passed into the preaching of Christ. For Jesus, too, repentance is the prerequisite of salvation, the gateway to the Kingdom. He indeed came to call sinners to repentance, and told of the joy in heaven over one change of heart. Jesus, no less severely than John, could say, "Except ye repent, ye shall all . . . perish".

In spite of this, the demand for repentance is well-nigh absent from modern Christianity. The twentieth-century gospel concerns comfort, integration, adjustment to life — not revolution, not ethical conversion, not penitence or judgement. John finds no place in our promotional programmes. The warnings of Jesus we silently ignore. Too much insistence upon repentance plays havoc with campaign results!

Yet in our hearts we know that we are wrong. Here is the basis of an ethical Christianity that really *saves* the sinner, not by easing his conscience but by changing his attitudes and conduct; saving him not only from hell but from sinning. The world and the Church and the Christian would be safer and stronger for the surgical message of John, divinely appointed precursor to the healing grace of Christ.

III

But would the modern world listen to a message so forbidding, or even the modern Church? Unexpectedly, the answer is provided in the figure of John himself.

To say that the wilderness prophet captured the imagination of Jewry is to say too little. Crowds flocked out to his preaching. The nation was divided; while the leaders questioned his message and his baptism, the people accorded him the highest of all titles — "prophet of God". Finding it impossible to believe or to ignore him, Herod the king put John in prison. Thirty years later and five hundred miles away Paul found a coterie of his disciples still keeping alive their master's memory. His impact upon Jewry was immense, and after his death his influence spread far and deep.

For this there were two reasons. Men *felt* his authority. John did not rely upon Scriptural learning or insight, or adhere to conventional Jewish teaching, or seek the support of rabbis and scribes. He spoke to the people of his time in the language of his time about the concerns of his time, as had the prophets before him: and he spoke with the relevance and power of a spokesman of God. Men felt this man was true. The whole argument that raged about him concerned this question of authority — was it of heaven, or of men. Until we find place again in our modern Christian work for that personal, direct, original authority of men called of God to speak for Him, no progress, or power, or unity, is possible.

Nevertheless authority was clothed with self-effacement. John's words were harsh, his message stern, his language forthright: his was no retiring personality, giving ground before his critics and yielding to opposition. Yet he knew his place. In comparison with Jesus, he was nothing.

John himself insists he is but friend of the Bridegroom, graciously privileged to attend the feast; just a pointing finger, marked "Behold!"; just a candle of God in a dark time, content to burn till daybreak, then to be forgotten; just a voice crying in the wilderness. "Unworthy am I, even to stoop before him to loosen his shoes. He must increase, I must decrease!"

That spirit and attitude fits ill into any publicity campaign. Strange poster-slogan, or radio signature-line: "I must decrease — I am nothing!" Here is no personality-promotion, no cult of the star performer; here, it seems to us, is the very negation, the plain denial, of authority. Yet nothing is more certain than this: until the world sees in the Church and in her spokesmen this combination of authority with humility, this plain speech unafraid and sure, together with an unselfseeking spirit of devotion, it will not listen to any message — least of all one calling for repentance.

IV

It would be unfaithful to John to neglect to glance at the figure of Jesus as John depicts Him. The portrait of Christ which the prophet presents is like all else — stern, forthright, and challenging. Jesus is "the mighty One". with power to save, to scourge, to convict, to judge. He is the "threshing Christ", sifting out the hearts of men as grain from chaff. He is the Woodman whose axe is laid already at the root of worthless trees. But He is also the Bridegroom, through whom delight and joy in the banquet of God's Kingdom comes to men. And He is the Lamb that beareth upon Himself and so beareth away the sin of the world.

As his later question sent to Jesus from the prison shows, John did not fully understand the Christ as yet. But his portrait of Jesus is vivid, striking, and — so far as it goes — true. John was a worthy herald of the King, with a perennial message which neither Church nor world can yet ignore. "Prepare ye the way of the Lord. Repent! For the world's King cometh."

7 Revelations at the Riverside

"Then cometh Jesus from Galilee to Jordan unto John to be baptised of him."   Matthew 3:13

THE FLASH-POINTS of history, it may truly be said, are always moments of creative coincidence. Converging trends and influences are confronted with a sudden event which illumines a whole era. Out of the seemingly undirected chain of causes and effects emerges a pattern which in the mind of thinker or hero, leader or saint, attains to understanding, shapes some crucial decision, and history turns a corner.

This happens, more often than not, because the outward shaping of the time and the inward development of the human spirit have *met* in some great soul, in whom the meaning of the age is represented and the importance of the time is crystallised.

Such a moment was reached when Jesus stood before John in the Jordan river. John represented the agelong spiritual development of Israel, the profound moral education of the Jewish people, the ardent hope persistently nourished by apocalyptist and prophet. In his person and message, despair of man and hope in God are significantly intertwined.

In Jesus, on the other hand, a deeper kind of preparation had reached its climax in the fashioning of a mind alert to every truth of God, a soul alive to every movement of God's Spirit, a will obedient to every command of the eternal Father, a heart in love with God. The call of God through John found Jesus ready, and the outcome was inevitable. As Jesus went down into the baptismal waters and rose to see the heavens opened and the Spirit descending like a dove upon Him, the angels themselves might hear the page of history being turned.

I

It was a surprise to John that Jesus sought his baptism. Just what gave John some hint of the truth about the Master we are not told, but he protested: "I have need to be baptised

of thee, and comest thou to me?" Jesus replied, "Allow it
to be so now, for thus it becometh us to fulfil all righteousness". And the reply is very significant.

Just as Jesus had already shared the home-life, toil, and
discipline of growth of those He came to save, so now He
shares the quickened expectation and awakening hope that
runs through Galilee. He is sure that John is a prophet,
and his baptism is "from heaven": that is enough. Publicly
He identifies Himself with the new religious movement,
lending the weight of His assent to the call for righteousness
which John was sounding, the hope of the Kingdom which
John was stirring. The movement was plainly born of God's
Spirit and attested by God's blessing: inevitably therefore
it claimed the Lord's allegiance. It is right to perform all
that is "righteous", to leave nothing undone that has God's
approval. So Jesus is baptised.

Jesus, that is to say, allied Himself with the best in His
generation. He would not hold aloof from the movements
and aspirations that, so far as they went, strove in right
directions. Of course, He knew the insufficiency of the
Baptist's message, the inadequacy of repentance without
spiritual rebirth: He was aware that John's ministry was too
negative, too full of threatening. But, though not perfect, it
was good; while not complete and final, it was true. And
Jesus gave to John His personal support.

The implication for ourselves is obvious.

II

As so frequently occurs, the immediate, obvious step of
obedience to God's call, resolutely and sincerely taken, leads
but further. Baptism at the hands of John became for Jesus
a vehicle expressing all His yieldedness to the Father's will,
all His dedication to whatever the Father would appoint for
Him. He rises from the water in an attitude of prayerful
waiting upon God, and then happens for Jesus what had
happened for none other of John's candidates: the heaven
is opened, the voice of God speaks to His soul, the Spirit
descends to rest upon Him in its fulness.

The Voice addresses Jesus in terms at once of approval
and of affirmation, charged with the most profound signifi-

cance: "Thou art my beloved Son, in whom I am well pleased". Into that brief sentence is packed, first, the highest possible assurance of Jesus' eternal Sonship, the unique relationship to God which sets Him forever apart from all other men. Secondly, and in consequence, the words recognise His messianic destiny and task, echoing the second Psalm. Thirdly, the second phrase designates Jesus as the long foretold Servant of Jehovah, God's Elect in whom He takes delight; but whom it will please the Lord to bruise, for He will bear the sin of many.

All that had hitherto developed within Christ's soul, growing with His growing, clarifying with His increasing wisdom and grace, is now — at any rate — perfectly, finally clear. Son, Messiah, Servant, He stands ready for all that God will ask of Him — or do with Him. From this moment onwards the inner assurance of Jesus is never once shaken. His baptism has set God's unchallengeable seal upon who Christ is.

At the same time, His baptism left Jesus endowed with everything necessary for His work. Hitherto, the Spirit's presence in His life might be said to have been a personal experience of His own; henceforth it is also an official endowment, a seal upon His commission as Messiah, a solemn anointing increasingly evident in the authority of His teaching, the immovable assurance of His Sonship, the clarity of His purpose, the singleness of His devotion, the transcendence of His claims, the power of His deeds, the absoluteness of His demands. A degree of power not needed at the carpenter's bench is now to be manifest in Him "without measure", for ministry, for conflict, and for suffering.

Jesus never returned to the seclusion of the Nazareth home. His baptism involved the final renunciation of security and privacy, the irrevocable acceptance of the divine call, the total dedication to the destiny which God's purpose determined for Him. The Jordan was His Rubicon. His baptism was a fitting close to all His preparation, a magnificent, exciting inauguration of His work.

III

As we reflect on the suggestions and the implications of Christ's baptism, seeing it now in the light of Calvary, it becomes apparent that Jesus came to baptism not only as any earnest Jew might come, responding to John's message, but as sharing in a deeper sense the predicament of man. For all but He John's baptism was "of repentance, unto remission of sins". As Jesus shared with men in the pious hopes of His generation, so He stood in with them in all the sin and rebelliousness which made those hopes unsure. Such is the significance of His baptism *for Christian faith*.

In His baptism, as in all else, we see the Master identify Himself with sinful men. The sinless Christ going down to a sinner's baptism provides an outstanding instance of the whole process of redemption. He takes His stand by the side of those He came to save, making their shame His shame, their burden His burden, their debt His responsibility. Here as everywhere He is content to be numbered with transgressors, and called the Friend of sinners. That is the gospel of His baptism: the loving identification of Christ with us in need that we might be identified with Him in grace and power and glory.

The significance of Christ's baptism *for Christian life* is plain. Ideally, our baptism ought to mean for us — at reverent distance — what His baptism meant for Him. The world has desperate need of committed, dedicated men, of declared allegiance and confessed vocation to the spiritual life. Our baptism, also, should mean a definite and irrevocable taking of sides with God's work in our generation, a ready and resolute dedication to whatsoever shall follow of service, conflict, or suffering.

No less surely the world has desperate need of men assured and equipped for spiritual battle, men baptised with the Spirit of Jesus and endued with power from on high. The baptism of the Spirit is the prime necessity of present-day Christianity; and when our baptism is made to enshrine the renunciation, the obedience, the dedication, the resolve, which His baptism implied, then there will follow a similar divine endowment.

God ever answers faith with assurance, surrender with joy, seeking with finding, obedience with blessing, dedication with equipment, consecration with the gift of His Spirit. The promises attached to baptism in the New Testament shame our too little faith; the proffered gifts are not received because too often we are unaware that they are ours. Yet so long as grace shall last it is not too late to see our own baptism in the light of His, to lay hold of all God offers in the gospel, to resolve that we, too, shall live, committed, dedicated, assured, endued, unto all the will of God.

8 Paths to a Throne

"And he was there in the wilderness forty days tempted."
Mark 1:13

DR. JAMES STALKER used to say that in the matter of temptation people were divided into six classes. All were tempted: the tree of the knowledge of good and evil stands in the midst of the garden, where all paths meet. But not all react alike.

Three classes on the left include those who are tempted and fall; three classes on the right those who are tempted and win through. In the first class on the left are those who, playing with temptation, are in perpetual danger; in the second, those who fall, their minds stained, consciences seared, names dishonoured; in the third, those who, having fallen, now tempt others.

On the right, in the first class are those who are tempted and manfully resist, with difficulty; in the second those who are tempted and overcome, finding victory in Christ; in the third, those who were tempted, who overcame, and now are the friends and counsellors of all weaker, storm-tossed souls.

Far to the right again, stands Jesus.

I

Jesus was tempted. The evangelists record it, Jesus described it. It was no pretence: ministering angels testify to its intensity, and sweat as drops of blood tell of its cost. It is true that Jesus seems ever to have been out of range of the coarser temptations that afflict most men. His temptations came always from without, never from within His own nature. And the issue was never in doubt: He shook off the temptation from His soul with clear and prompt decision that left not the slightest stain or scar. He remains "the Holy One of God".

But the completeness of His victory must not throw doubt upon His struggle, or make us question the story He Himself tells. The testing of the moral fibre of His soul and the depth

47

of His consecration that came upon Him in the wilderness and afterwards, was fierce and painful — all the more so to a nature sensitive as His. "We have not a high priest which cannot be touched with the feelings of our infirmities; but one who was in all points tempted like as we are, yet without sin."

II

Remembering that Jesus Himself described the wilderness temptation, we shall not be surprised at the use of symbolic imagery to portray an experience essentially inward and spiritual; nor at the intimate relation of the temptation-story to His baptism. The *avenue* of each temptation is a common frailty of human nature; but the *ground* of each attack is doubt of what at the baptism had been affirmed — "*If* thou be the Son of God . . . " and the *issue* in each case is directly concerned with His vocation as Messiah. The tempting suggestions laid before Jesus are all alternative paths to a throne. Satan offers three short cuts to His Kingdom, by-passing the cross.

The avenue of the first temptation is the innocent appetite of a hungry man. It serves as type of all those evil suggestions which approach man through his physical nature, enticing him to satisfy a lower hunger at the price of a higher one, to set the demands of the flesh above those of the spirit. The craving is natural, the circumstances extenuating: "there's no harm in it!" But "man shall not live by bread alone". He cannot direct his life by his lower impulses without sacrificing the higher. Life and security lie not in satisfying the physical but in sanctifying it to the spiritual ends for which alone the physical exists.

Yet the issue raised is wider. Moses had given the people manna in the wilderness, and Messiah is expected to do the same. So, after the feeding of five thousand there was a concerted move in Galilee "to take Jesus by force and make him king". A kingdom might easily be won that way: "give the people what they want!" But Jesus consistently refused a theocratic welfare-state where material prosperity should be the promised reward for spiritual submission.

Not all Christ's followers have so firmly rejected that essentially worldly dream.

III

Ambition may be as innocent as hunger: equally it may become the last infirmity of noble minds. When it stoops to ruthlessness, injustice, carelessness of others, or ministers to avarice and pride, then it corrupts the soul. To gain the kingdoms of the world by subservience to the world's ways is to be destroyed by one's own success.

But had not Jesus just been commissioned to receive the kingdoms of this world? To be offered them on condition that He fall down and worship the "prince of this world" was to be tempted in line with His life's whole purpose. So the party of Zealots would overthrow Rome by Rome's own weapons. Let Messiah out-Caesar Tiberias, and rule the world the way the world understands!

Throughout His ministry Jesus faced and resisted this suggestion: in Galilee by insisting on the turning of the other cheek; in Gethsemane by the remonstrance, "Put up thy sword", and the refusal to pray for the intervention of the angels; at Pilate's judgement seat by the declaration, "My kingdom is not of this world, else would my servants fight".

In Christ's eyes, the end, however desirable and good, can never sanctify the means. Violence, hatred, militarism are the devil's forces, and cannot build God's Kingdom. Only service, love and sacrifice can win the allegiance of men's hearts, and without that Christ will not rule. "Thou shalt worship the Lord thy God" and serve Him in His own way: only so can His work be done. That answer made the cross inevitable.

It still does.

IV

The suggestion that Jesus cast Himself from the Temple roof, relying on the ancient promise of protection, is typical of all the temptations that come through the avenue of religion and the intellectual life. Such is the sin of the Pharisee vaingloriously presuming upon God's favour; the sin of the hypocrite who goes his own wilful way quoting texts to justify himself; the sin of intellectual pride putting the Almighty to its own petty tests to try God's faithfulness — which is infidelity; the sin of the religiously ostentatious, loving the praise of men more than the praise of God.

The seeds of all such attitudes are contained in this third temptation.

But again, for Jesus the issue is wider. Christ yearned for the multitude, longed to shepherd them. The spectacle of His descent unhurt from Temple turret to crowded court-yard would surely convince many of His claims. Besides, tradition declared that "when Messiah is revealed, he comes and stands upon the roof of the Holy Place: then will he announce . . . the time of your redemption is come". A programme of supernatural "evidences" would evoke untold enthusiasm among the common people.

The response of Jesus was brusque: "an *evil* and *adulterous* generation seeketh after a sign!" — that is, a generation incapable of reading the true moral signs of the times. Throughout His ministry Jesus refused to force faith by miracles, or do wonders merely for advertisement or self-display. Rule based upon supernatural powers would be far less than the Kingdom of freely obedient hearts that God desired. For that, the cross was necessary.

Thus one by one the current ideas of what Messiah should do are reviewed and rejected: bribery by material prosperity and bread, alliance with the world's own forces to subdue the world, the spectacle of signs and wonders. As Jesus leaves the wilderness retreat His mind is made up: it is by teaching, healing, compassion and friendship, service and sacrifice, that the Kingdom must be built and the obedience of men be won. The short cuts are scorned. The path from the baptism to the throne must run past Golgotha. For Him, as for us, "no cross, no crown".

V

Contemporary implications aside, what has the temptation and triumph of Jesus to offer us in our own moral struggles?

We may learn something from His uncompromising spirit. Temptation is inevitable, but to seek it out is wrong, to play with it is stupid, to "make provision for it" by permitting situations to arise in which one is left open to its power is to deserve defeat. Temptation is the crucible of character, and so the crux of destiny: only fools sport on the edge of the precipice.

We may learn much from Christ's well-armoured soul.

The solemn dedication of His baptism, the long-established habit of prayer, the mind stored with God's truth, these are His weapons against evil. An empty house, He later said, is a standing invitation to devils to enter and defile it. The conquering soul is he who overcomes temptation before it arises, putting on the whole armour of God before the trumpet sounds for battle.

We may learn most from Christ's companionship in all our conflicts. "In that he himself hath suffered, being tempted, he is able to succour them that are tempted." The momentary prayer, the swift turning of the mind to Him, the breathing of His name, calling upon His strength, thus facing temptation with the triumphant Christ, are the simple secrets in which lies all our hope of growing in His likeness and sharing in His victory.

But we shall learn none of these things properly unless we begin with Jesus in the wilderness. Unless, that is, we learn with Him to turn resolutely away from all the proffered short cuts and specious excuses, the subtle side-tracking that would represent the Christian life as ever on the emotional Mount of Transfiguration, and never called to climb the moral mount of self-crucifixion. The spiritualised hedonism, or "enlightened self-interest" that passes for some modern Christianity will not stand the analysis of Christ's temptation experience. A specious, persuasive, prosperity-loving, success-hunting, publicity-plugging religion is very far removed from the utter dedication to the *painful* will of God which marked Christ's spirit as He left the wilderness. But then, He overcame, where we too often merely evade. He achieved salvation: we so often are only concerned that our little selfish souls be "richly blessed"!

9 Nazareth Manifesto

*"The Spirit of the Lord is upon me, because he hath anointed
me to preach the gospel to the poor; he hath sent me to
heal the brokenhearted, to preach deliverance to the captives, and recovering of sight to the blind, to set at liberty
them that are bruised, to preach the acceptable year of
the Lord."*   Luke 4:18-19

FLATTERY and threats are equally perilous to the conscientious preacher. At Nazareth Jesus met both. True, it was
His hometown, and a prophet in his own country expects
suspicion and envy. But gracious words and winsome manner won golden opinions from some in that synagogue
congregation as Jesus expounded Isaiah 61, the lesson for
the day.

As often happens, the criticism when it came missed
the really big issues, and concentrated on matters com-
paratively insignificant. What troubled the Sabbath peace
was Christ's reminder of God's interest in a *Gentile* sufferer,
God's use of a *Gentile* widow to shelter and protect a
prophet unwelcome in Israel. That His argument for God's
universal love rested on their own Scriptures and was unanswerable, but increased their fury. Disturbed about this, they
missed altogether the real implications of His far-reaching sermon: the first recorded definition of the long-expected
and now imminent messianic Kingdom.

I

The central theme of that Nazareth announcement was
His programme and its purpose. Had the congregation
known it, they were witnessing at once the fulfilment and
the re-interpretation of all their agelong dreams. Behind
them, as they listened, lay the treasured expectations
nourished by prophets and seers of coming dominion and
glory for Israel. Behind Jesus, as He spoke, lay the experience
of the baptism and the penetrating reappraisal of Messiah's
work that was the meaning of the temptation. The issue of
that sermon was to prove as fateful for them as it was for

Him. In that quiet village service a new idea was coming to birth which would transform forever mankind's conception of the purposes of God.

In Christ's swift, persuasive sentences three things dear to Jewry were being set aside. The privileged position of the learned, the elect, the wealthy, and the wellborn was quietly destroyed. The heavy yoke of the all-sufficient, all-dominating law, with its multitudinous burdens translating godliness into bondage, was removed. The dreams of political conquest and revenge were dissolved away. Instead, into the centre of His picture move the poor, the brokenhearted, the captive, the blind, and the bruised. These are to form Christ's Kingdom and His friends, and "good news", comfort, liberation, light, and healing are to be foundations of His throne.

Grace and not judgement, freedom in place of bondage, gladness and healing instead of bitterness and war are to be marks of Messiah's reign. Concern for "the poor" will bear fruit in charity and justice. Care for "the brokenhearted" will bring back tenderness and hope to a cruel world. "Deliverance of captives" implies the end of tyranny and oppression, the emancipation of all who are enslaved. "Sight for the blind" includes the vision of God and the inward illumination of the everlasting truth for a world groping in darkness and error. "Healing for the bruised" involves the righting of all earth's wrongs and the protection of the defenceless against misuse of power.

Not many in Israel looked for such things as signs of the messianic Kingdom. But these define Christ's purpose and dictate His programme. They revolutionise henceforth all human understanding of what God is after in the earth, what sort of world it is that, in His name, we strive to build.

II

We are here at the heart of *Christ's message and its meaning.* "Jesus came into Galilee preaching the gospel of the kingdom of God and saying, The time is fulfilled, the kingdom of God is at hand." The gospel of Jesus *is* the gospel of the Kingdom. This is the message His disciples were twice commissioned to proclaim; this is the "good news" that "must be preached in all the world"; this is the message which Paul declared, "another King . . . the gospel of the kingdom". And well nigh all Christ's sayings are rays of this outshining hope.

Essentially, the *meaning of the Kingdom* is the kingly rule of the Father-God in the hearts of willing men. Already the will of God is done in heaven: it is to be so done on earth and then the Kingdom is here. "It cometh not with observation", but is "within you"; yet by that very centrality and inwardness it must inevitably spread like leaven, grow like seed, shine like light, cleanse and preserve like salt, working outwards from the centre until all life's circumference is under God's sway. The first surrender, establishing the Kingdom in the soul, is individual and spiritual; its immediate effects are also social and secular; its ultimate outcome will be universal and eternal: God will be all in all.

To enter this life under divine direction is to find peace and joy, relief from anxiety, release from fear. It is to come upon treasure awaiting discovery in the fields of experience. It is to find in life's busy market place a goodly pearl, priceless and beautiful. It is to sit at God's table with the great in all ages, sharing a royal marriage-feast through all one's days.

The new wine of the Kingdom is a blessedness, intoxicating and free, shared by all in whose heart the will of God is regnant. Theirs is the marvel of the Kingdom's gladness, the deep peace of life surrendered to the hand of God, the quiet strength of life rooted in the will of God, the abiding joy of life dedicated to the aim of God, the spiritual victory of life lived royally in the presence of the King. The message of the Kingdom is the world's best news yet!

The *men of the Kingdom* are known by the quality of their personal life. They sit lightly to this world's goods, in spirit consenting to poverty if God so will, but possessing the Kingdom. They are saddened by the evil around them, but comforted in God. A reverent humility preserves their meekness under provocation, yet they possess the earth. They hunger and thirst after righteousness, but not in vain. They use whatever power falls to their hands with gentleness and generosity, as themselves also hoping for mercy.

The hearts of the men of the Kingdom preserve their

purity, and see God in all their life. They are set, like God's own heart, on making peace. They meet unflinchingly a persecuting world, aware that this is the hall-mark of the godly in every generation and sure of the reward laid up for all who love God more than life. Such standards are high: but such are Christ's kind of people for Christ's kind of world.

The *manner of the Kingdom* is expounded in epigram and parable, precept and challenge. Purity and truth, service and love are the royal laws. Efficient and ready consecration of one's talents; compassion towards the hungry, the naked, the sick, the imprisoned; active intervention befriending all found wounded and bleeding on the roadside of life; constancy in prayer; readiness to forgive; freedom from the anxiety that undermines the heart — such are the outward signs that God reigns within the soul.

Thus the Kingdom Jesus preached is not primarily an historical event but a spiritual experience, though it works out in historical patterns and power for Christlike action. It is not primarily a world revolution but a personal possession, though it radically changes every life it touches and through obedient men affects the widest world affairs. It is not primarily a social ideal but a central relationship of the soul to its King, though again it has definite social implications.

The Kingdom begins with the enthronement of the King. It is sustained, and grows, in heartfelt repentance towards the self-willed past, in steadfast faith in the love that so wisely rules, in constantly renewed surrender to the rule that so unchangeably loves.

III

Not all this was said at Nazareth, of course: but all was implied in the far-reaching re-interpretations which Jesus imposed on the messianic expectations of His day. Yet even this is not the most startling aspect of that Sabbath sermon. More disturbing still was the concentration of His programme upon *Himself and His invitation*. "This day is this scripture fulfilled in your ears", and the Scripture had described the coming of the Servant to set men free. "The Spirit of the Lord is upon *me*" He declared, "because he hath anointed *me* . . . . " A third time is the implication underlined: "To preach the acceptable year of the Lord". The year awaited has now arrived — because He is there! Scripture, Spirit, and sign all indicate Himself. In His presence among men the Kingdom had come.

Here lies the critical, crucial fact, the provocative, divisive truth: the Kingdom is His, it is present where He is acknowledged. "Come unto me" is His invitation, "and ye shall find rest . . . . Believe on me, and ye shall know the truth, and the truth shall make you free . . . . Come, that ye might have life!" It is as simple as that. God's Kingdom has begun wherever the King is welcomed.

> *Blest are all that touch His sceptre,*
> *Blest are all that own His sway;*
> *Freed from sin, that worst of tyrants,*
> *Rescued from its galling chain;*
> *Saints and Angels —*
> *All who know Him bless His reign!*

10 Recruiting Colleagues

"And he ordained twelve, that they should be with him, and that he might send them forth."   Mark 3:14

INTO THE FINAL paragraph of the first chapter of John's Gospel are gathered a group of people as assorted and familiar as might fill any railroad waiting room, or pass in five minutes on a busy sidewalk. Manual workers, conspicuous by soiled clothes and hardened hands, include some strongly built, loud-voiced, emotional, and others small, wiry men, quiet, good listeners, often overborne but reliable and tough. Just such were Peter and Andrew.

In neater clothes are office-men, with education, facts, and understanding in their conversation to betray their different training. Some have private sources of information, or friends in high places, and tend to become dogmatic, intolerant, anxious to impress. Just such was John.

The cautious, shrewd professional man talks little. He sits silent, absorbed in reading, or engages in brief, guarded conversation; he is intelligent, courteous, but withdrawn. Such a man was Philip. In a seat by himself, with Testament open on his knee and a badge in his coat, is a "religious type", serious, aloof, dreamy — or possibly too aggressively religious — either way he is awkward to get to know, a poor mixer. Such probably was Nathanael.

So Jesus might come into any waiting room, queue, or bar, and find His men. What ordinary flesh and blood they are! Not a priest or scribe or Pharisee among them! We lose a great deal by giving them robes and haloes, and calling them "Saint Peter, Saint John".

> *He raised not an army for to fight*
> *And force religion, but did men invite*
> *By gentle means. Twelve of the simpler sort*
> *Served to make up His train and kept His court.*

The mighty, moving thing that happened in Palestine long ago and reverberates still through all the centuries, happened to ordinary folk. It can happen to us.

And what varied folk they were. Too easily we assume that Christians are, or should be, of one pattern, cast in a mould that corresponds as nearly as possible with our own experience. It is salutary to recall that Christ's message is not addressed to just one type, nor does it produce a dull uniformity of outlook or of character. It enhances and refines the best in each, increasing the natural variety of human personality to the enrichment of all.

Christ's twelve had only one natural quality in common: their youthfulness. They differed in temperament and interests — Simon was an ardent nationalist, Matthew a minor civil servant, Peter impetuous and uncouth, John thoughtful, though "thunderous", Andrew simple and believing, Thomas a hardheaded melancholy soul, Philip a curious, enquiring mind.

A like diversity has marked the Christian Church in every generation. Soldiers, scholars, statesmen, reformers, poets, artists, thinkers, and men of daring jostle each other in the story of the gospel. Who shall find easily the common factor that unites Augustine with Bernard and Francis, Luther with Damien, Wesley with Kagawa, Bergraav with Billy Graham?

Christianity, it has been said, has a nose of wax; it is a mask for many faces. Maybe so, but it has a single heart of gold, and a uniting love for Christ. *The mighty, moving thing that happened in Palestine long ago and reverberates still through all the centuries, happened to various kinds of folk*. It can happen to our kind.

It is not less significant that the chosen twelve varied as widely in spiritual stature. None was outstanding in quickness of perception, or eagerness to obey. Parables had to be simply explained, old lessons relearned. Thoughts better left unspoken were often blurted out. They criticised each other, tried to overreach each other, were sometimes jealous, brusque, ill-tempered. They slept when He needed their company, quarrelled when He was heavy-hearted, forsook Him and fled when the crisis came upon Him. One denied, another doubted, a third betrayed.

These were no spiritual experts. They were called as they were, for what He still could make of them. In the school of Christ there is room, and welcome, for the slow of heart, the dull of mind, the erring, the weak, so long as each be willing to learn — disciples indeed. *The mighty, moving thing that happened in Palestine long ago and reverberates still through all the centuries, happened to people of varied spiritual attainment, or none at all.* It can happen to us.

And the diversity of the men is matched by the variety of their experience. John and Andrew reached the truth step by step, approaching by way of the Baptist's preaching, making their own enquiry, receiving His "Come, and see". Peter was hustled to Christ by an importunate brother, not seeking but searched, and held —

Thou hast the art on't, Peter, and canst tell
To cast thy nets on all occasions well:
When Christ calls, and thy nets would have thee stay,
To cast them well's to cast them quite away!

With Philip no one intervened. He was sought out, called, graciously but imperatively, and he had only to obey. Then Philip found Nathanael and brought him to Jesus, who read his inmost thought, commenting upon his scriptural meditation beneath the fig tree by offering Himself a new Jacob's ladder, linking heaven and earth. Nathanael immediately capitulated to such insight, and such claim.

John found a Friend to love, Andrew a Lord to serve and share with others, Peter a Master to reduce his turbulent nature to ordered strength. Philip discovered a Teacher, Nathanael the inmost truth of God, Matthew a Comrade attractive and commanding. Soon, all were to find Him Redeemer and King. For Christ is all this and more. Only "with *all* the saints" can any *one* comprehend the height, breadth, length, and depth of Christ or understand His love. *The mighty, moving thing that happened in Palestine long ago and reverberates still through all the centuries, happened in varied ways.* It can happen to us in our individual way, beginning just where we are.

II

Yet beneath the variety of men and motives, of experience and response, there lies a consistent purpose. *The twelve were called to a great companionship,* "to be with him", living under His spell, learning His secret, sharing His spirit. This was the essence of their "discipling". They were to concentrate exclusively on "learning Christ", to lay their minds alongside His mind, their hearts alongside His, listening, watching, learning, loving. Yoked for three years with Him, they were to be searched and stretched and stimulated until in truth they grew like Him.

Men later remarked about these men, seeking the explanation of their power, that they "had been with Jesus". This is still the highest ideal of Christian living: to grow like Christ; and this is still the secret of its motive power: to live so close to Christ that the quality of His spirit infects one's own.

Yet even that high goal could be no end within itself. *The twelve were called to a great commission,* "that he might send them forth". The gospel was to be written in their redeemed lives, and they must go forth into the world where men might read its message. Doctrine, ethics, vision, challenge —all were enshrined in "living witnesses", both mouthpieces and exemplars of His saving grace. In them He multiplied Himself, sending them forth to preach and to heal "whithersoever he himself would go". In them He perpetuated Himself, as they continued His work and ministry after His ascension. In them He expressed and explained Himself, not in words or ritual, but in the impress left upon their hearts.

Here, in embryo, was the Christian Church, a *corps d'élite,* a spiritual pressure group, not brilliant or perfect, but dedicated, enlightened, keen, determined, and in love with Christ. What might not Jesus do with such a band again!

It seems incredible that even the Son of God would not try to save the world *alone.* He called men into the task with Him. To His atoning work for a world in sin, no human hand or heart can add the merest mite. But His cause on earth He has committed to the men in every generation called to be with Him and to be sent forth, equipped with His gospel, empowered by His Spirit, sustained by His presence, to the end of the age. *The mighty, moving thing that happened in Palestine so long ago and reverberates still through all the centuries, happens yet* — wherever men will hear His simple call, "Come, follow me!"

> *In simple trust like theirs who heard*
> *Beside the Syrian sea,*
> *The gracious calling of the Lord,*
> *Let us, like them, without a word*
> *Rise up and follow Thee.*

Ministry that expounds salvation

Miracles with a meaning
Conversations with a purpose
Never man spake like this Man
Truth in a tale
Character immaculate

simple compassion. His tender words to the bereaved and the afflicted, His eloquent touch for the leper and the blind, His kindly authority in speaking with the demented and insane, His patience to establish communication with the deaf-mute, His great effort at secrecy, where public knowledge would disgrace a newly-wed couple or create insuperable difficulties for a child, all reveal a heart sharing to the full our human sorrows and carrying with deepest understanding the burden of our pain.

Our scientific age can ill afford to dispense with the wellspring of human tenderness which is opened afresh in every generation by the compelling example of Christ's compassion.

A second motive underlying the miracle-ministry is the assertion of divine victory. Evil in all its forms, physical and mental no less than moral and spiritual, was to Christ an intrusion into God's world. It has no rightful place where God is King. In the corporate responsibility of the race, suffering, affliction and sorrow may fall most severely upon the least ill-deserving, and handled with courage and grace they may serve to discipline souls to otherwise impossible heights of human character. But essentially they do not belong in God's perfect plan.

Wherever in Christ's person the frontiers of God's Kingdom were extended, therefore, there inevitably the frontiers of evil were forced back. When God's will is done on earth as it is done in heaven, earth becomes heaven, and sorrow and sighing flee away. That is the inspiration and enduring confidence of every endeavour to defeat evil and banish suffering from God's world.

Reinforcing compassion for the afflicted and zeal for God's purpose of perfection was the profound assumption, natural to the Hebrew mind and reaffirmed by Jesus, that salvation is for the whole man. Later Greek thought, like modern thought, divided personality into body, mind, and soul (or spirit), and made religion the concern only of the immaterial elements in man. To Biblical thought, the body, too, is God's and is redeemed, and will be raised again.

So Christ desired the reasonable, enlightened mind in the healthy, unhindering body, a disciplined, developed, and complete personality for His instrument. Unless all the man is saved, salvation is incomplete.

And unless faith receives this whole salvation, faith is incomplete. Far more than we realise, the health of body and mind is linked to health of spirit, and He who is "Saviour of the body" is its Healer and Sustainer too. We cannot dictate His will for our lives, but on the other hand we must let Him do all that He wants to do, for us and in us —

> *Just as I am, poor, wretched, blind,*
> *Sight, riches, healing of the mind,*
> *Yea, all I need, in Thee to find,*
> *O Lamb of God, I come.*

II

But deeds do not only accomplish things, they express things; and all the acts of Jesus are dramatically eloquent. So John always represents the miracles of Christ as *signs*. They are acted parables, which beyond their immediate purpose portray the saving grace of Christ on deeper levels of experience.

When Jesus heals the blind, He demonstrates His claim to be the Light of the world, so that those who follow Him no longer walk in darkness. When Jesus cures the lame, He portrays His power to set wandering feet in ways of righteousness and love. Unstopping deaf ears, He shows how He can bring again the Word of God to souls long unreceptive and insensitive. Feeding the multitude, He implies that He is the Bread of life.

The fevered are calmed by the same touch that soothes the fretful life; the storm is stilled on the sea as in the soul; the wasting, ebbing life is stayed, restored to strength and use again; the paralysed in body and in soul are alike set gloriously free.

Demented, disordered minds find sanity through the same gracious power that finds men lost in mazes of unbelief. Physical or moral lepers, equally, are cleansed by the touch of Jesus. The same liberating love makes the dumb to speak and silent, inarticulate souls break forth in song and testimony. The dead are raised at the word of the Prince of Life. On every level, at His command, the water of life is changed to wine.

So every deed of wonder is a concrete illustration of redeeming grace, breaking in upon wasted, fettered, hungry, darkened, silent souls with light and life, with health and power, with liberty and cleansing and salvation. And as He was, so is He yet.

> *The healing of His seamless dress*
> *Is by our beds of pain;*
> *We touch Him in life's throng and press*
> *And we are whole again.*

III

The widest significance of the healing ministry of Jesus is revealed, however, by an unexpected incident. From his imprisonment the Baptist sent to Jesus a perplexed enquiry: "Art thou he that should come, or look we for another?" It was, fundamentally, a theological question, about the right title for Jesus and the true nature of His Kingdom. Jesus replied, not with a definition, but with news, a description of things happening: "Go and show John again . . . . The blind receive their sight, and the lame walk, the lepers are cleansed, and the deaf hear, the dead are raised up, and the poor have the gospel preached to them".

John had preached a Messiah with axe, flail, and fire of judgement. Instead he hears of a Messiah who "goes about doing good, and healing". Christ, and Kingdom, are far other than he expected, far other indeed than prophets and apocalyptists had foretold.

Yet there was fulfilment here, if John could see it, of the prophetic dream of a perfect world, a golden age. There is power here that confronts demonic forces and is victorious. There is more in Jesus than compassion, and healing: judgement would indeed fall on those who oppose Him — their opposition would be their judgement!

But for all that, John must learn, as we must learn, that the Kingdom of God is a Kingdom of active, relevant love, vicariously carrying and victoriously overcoming the ills and sorrows and shame of men. Christians cannot pass by on the other side: they must face and outface every evil in Christ's name, and assert God's rule.

For across the wide world, even yet, amid the rising nationalisms and reviving paganisms of East and South,

John's question is still being posed, sometimes wistfully, sometimes antagonistically, sometimes in simple perplexity: "Art thou, Christ, he that should come, or look we for another?" The only answer that will convince or satisfy, that is adequate to the question or worthy of the Christ, is the old answer of the Master.

We may tell them the story of the manger and the cross; we may offer them the Scriptures: what they still want to know is whether the stories are relevant to modern perplexities. They demand to be shown the truth made plain, the love made real, in significant *action*. They enquire whether Christianity makes any practical difference to war and peace, to starvation and plenty, to refugees, lepers, the ignorant, and the underprivileged. If the world is ever to accept our valuation of Jesus, we *must* show that where He rules hearts are made compassionate, evil is truly conquered, Christ's servants do a Christlike work; that where His Kingdom comes the blind see, the lame walk, the lepers are cleansed, and to the poor of the earth worthwhile good news is preached.

12 Conversations with a Purpose

*"Jesus answering said unto him, Simon, I have something
to say unto thee. And he saith, Master, say on."*

Luke 7:40

I

TALKING WITH OLD men about birth and new beginnings tends
always to wistfulness. Nicodemus could not understand how
time could run back, the mistakes of youth be cancelled, the
bonds of age and habit lose their grip, and life start over
again. "How *can* a man be born again when he is old?"

But Jesus knew that without rebirth there is no hope.
Said T. R. Glover, "Jesus loved men, but had no illusions
about them". Says the Fourth Gospel, "He knew what was in
man" — knew, that is, the heights and depths of human
nature, the weakness of the undisciplined flesh, the wickedness of the unregenerate heart.

With all who have truly measured the problem of evil,
Jesus understood that in spite of all that Nicodemus represented of learning, culture, social and religious status, man's
nature cannot, unaided, rise above its own level. That which
is born of the flesh is flesh, and remains flesh. To the "natural
man" the Kingdom of God is unthinkable, "he cannot see
it"; and unattainable, "he cannot enter it".

It is therefore a particularly foolish criticism of the
Christian ethic that it is "beyond human nature". Of course
it is. But human nature can be born anew, and from above,
becoming a new creature, in a new world, centred in God.
Man can be "born" of the baptismal water of repentance,
and "born" of the Holy Spirit, to a life wholly deriving from
God, sustained by grace, and tending towards eternity.

In such terms, profound and forthright, did Jesus explain
in private conversation the inmost truth of His programme
for the world, and the heart of His good news: the strict
necessity, and glorious opportunity, of personal regeneration.

II

Simon the Pharisee invited Jesus to his table. There came
a woman, seemingly belonging to the group of Christ's

friends, whose appearance betrayed a sinful life. She had come prepared to do Christ homage, but as she knelt before Him, emotion overwhelmed her, and in extremity of penitence and grief she wiped her falling tears from His feet with her own hair.

The Pharisee watched contemptuously. Prophets were expected to read character, and Jesus, if He were a prophet, should recoil from the defilement of her touch. Jesus evidently could not read hearts!

That judgement was suddenly shattered. An apparently innocent question about money-lending — ever of interest to the wealthy Pharisees — provoked a supercilious answer: of course the larger the debt the greater the gratitude if for some quixotic reason the debt be cancelled.

The bait taken, the trap was sprung. As neighbours, guests, and servants stood in shocked silence round the table, Jesus with quite unusual anger flayed the Pharisee's atrocious manners and disgraceful hospitality. "Did you see this woman, Simon? — you did not greet her! I came at your request, not mine, to this your table; but where are the simple courtesies a guest expects? She whom you despise can teach you lessons in civility. Her tears provide the water you thought unnecessary, her hair the towel you would not lend, her costly ointment the soothing oil that you withheld, her ceaseless kisses supply the want of your omitted welcome. Sinner she may be — but she is better aware of what is fitting than you are!"

In such words burns all Christ's passionate indignation against social snobbery and religious pride. But He has not done. "Look upon her love, Simon, how self-abasing, penitent, passionate — and remember your own words. The greatness of her love reveals the greatness of the pardon she has known. Then look upon yourself, who love little, and know the measure of your need!" Then, turning to the woman, Jesus said, "Thy faith hath saved thee, go in peace".

An exquisite, if surprising, incident. In another personal conversation Jesus has imparted a deep secret of His gospel. The *giver* of forgiveness is Himself; its *basis* is faith — just the coming to Him; the *sense* of forgiveness is peace, its *proof* is grateful love. By the moral dynamic of such love Christ will yet transform the world.

III

The rich young ruler possessed everything that compels attention — youth, wealth, excellent character, social prominence. Moreover, he was desperately in earnest. Such men do not run to kneel in public before a preaching carpenter without some urgent purpose.

His was no sinful heart, like Mary Magdalene's, or fettered like Augustine's, or fearful like Luther's, or burdened with great guilt like Bunyan's. Rather, he came dissatisfied, soul-hungry, asking for fuller and higher and more abundant *life*. He wanted a life transcendent and transfiguring, in harmony with the divine Spirit, in line with the divine purpose, impelled by the divine energy, in communion with the divine Father. He asked for life eternal, a quality of living that would last forever because rooted already among eternal things.

It was a serious request, and seriously answered. Yet the young man went away deeply *grieved* — a curious result.

For the first time he saw himself by other standards than his own, and all his confidence and pride were suddenly destroyed. His laborious keeping of the law, his struggles and victories, were in a moment set in a new light, devalued, the merest ABC of moral attainment, beside the demand of Jesus to "sell all . . . and give . . . . Come . . . follow me!" It was no more than Peter, John, and the rest had done; but it implied yielding up control, and consecration, and commitment. And it seemed too much.

Once more in private conversation, Jesus had presented the towering moral challenge of His gospel — devotion to the good of others, denial of the claims of self, dedication to the will of God. Knowing himself unwilling, yet realising that such was indeed the way to life eternal, the young man turned sadly away, humbled, chastened, self-exposed.

And Jesus let him go.

IV

At the wellhead in Samaria two tired people faced each other. One grown weary in service, the other worn out with sinning. Jesus was spent with toil for others, with strife against unbelief, with the nervous strain of His deep compassion. Virtue continually went out of Him: "being weary with his journey, he sat thus by the well".

The woman came in the burning sun to draw water, parched of soul, her life drained of healthy interests and emotions, over-stimulated by the sensual, a poor, worn, bedraggled, disillusioned creature for whom all the wells of joy had long run dry.

Jesus faced in her, as He faces in our own generation, deep spiritual weariness, boredom, premature agedness; the craving for stimulants — or sedatives — to make tolerable a life self-drained of inspiration, idealism, and faith. And He offered her, as He offers us, perpetual refreshment, an unfailing spring of inexhaustible and glorious life.

Their talk appears to drift, though in truth her evasions are no match for His sure insight. He asks refreshment, thus introducing the vital topic; she professes surprise at His approach, for He is a Jew. In answer He offers her refreshment, but she questions if He can supply it. Then plainly He invites her to share the secret of perennial refreshment within the soul.

She chooses to misunderstand, and Jesus then elicits the shameful truth of her career, because without confession the blight of sensuality upon her soul could not be lifted. Perceiving He is talking of religion, the woman now takes refuge in hackneyed questions about where and how men ought to worship. Jesus brings her back to the essentials of all worship, spirit and truth in contrast to her life of fleshliness and lies.

The woman's mind then flies to another evasion, the safely distant future, and problems of prophecy concerning Messiah. At once the Lord confronts her with the final, pointed challenge: "I that speak . . . am he!" At last convinced, all weariness lifted by confession, hope, and faith, she hurries back to the city with overflowing mind and heart while Jesus, all tiredness gone, greets the amazed disciples with the precept that doing the will of God is refreshment enough for faithful hearts.

In still another private conversation the Master had extended the supreme invitation of His gospel, the call to share already in the fulness of eternal life, living on adequate resources and perpetually replenished from within.

V

Among the great ones of the earth, only the very honest can afford to give themselves away in spontaneous table-talk. Only the very humble are willing to do so. To spend time and thought so freely for the benefit of individuals alone implies a whole range of value-judgements concerning people, concerning oneself, concerning the importance of personal relationship in a divided world.

The modern publicist or politician, too often even the modern evangelist, thinks only of the crowd, the weight of numbers, the far-ranging power of the large following. It is entirely characteristic of Jesus thus to sit talking to one or two; to interrupt history's most important journey — His journey to the cross — to eat with a tax-gatherer; to pause beside Bethesda for question and answer with the paralysed; to seek out in a day of peril the once-blind excommunicate to comfort him; to give time on the first Easter Day to conversation with a single erring soul.

When we know the mind of Jesus, such things seem natural and of course. And when one recalls the outcome, such private interviews with souls are understood — they are among the Lord's most powerful instruments in the redemption of the world.

13 Never Man Spake Like This Man

*"Then came the officers to the chief priests and Pharisees;
and they said unto them, Why have ye not brought him? The
officers answered, Never man spake like this man."*

John 7:45, 46

THE AUTHORS of this tribute were no uncultured peasants,
spell-bound by a glib-tongued demagogue — they were officials
of the Jewish Parliament, well used to listening to speeches.
Yet the eloquence of Jesus makes them disregard their orders.

Similarly charmed, the crowd pressed so eagerly upon
Him by the lakeside that prudence required a small boat wait
on Him that He might speak across the water from the
safety of the prow. A vast concourse, including women and
children, followed without food through a long eastern day
far into evening, lest any precious word of His be lost.

The synagogue congregation at Nazareth wondered greatly
at the gracious words He spoke, enquiring the secret of His
pulpit power. Peter spoke for literally thousands: "Lord, to
whom can we go? Thou hast the words of eternal life." Friend
and foe alike confess that never man spake like this Man.

I

One outstanding quality of Jesus' speech was His natural,
inherent, and assumed *authority*. Mark continually stresses
this. Others tell of whispered comments, comparing His
direct, innate authority with the endless quotations from
"authorities" cited by the Scribes.

Still more eloquent is the tribute of a centurion of the
Roman legions, trained to the habit of commanding speech:
"I *also* am a man set in authority". But equally significant
is the way Jesus makes pronouncements on matters commonly regarded as carrying direct divine sanction — the Sabbath,
forgiveness, and the Temple. And He gives similar authority,
in His own name, to disciples.

In two characteristics of Christ's speech it is still possible
to *feel* this impress of authority. One is His frequent "Verily,
verily, I say unto you . . .", echoing the divine "amen" of

ancient days, and the still more solemn "Thus saith the Lord" of prophetic utterances. The other is Christ's repeated challenge to the sacred Torah: "Ye have heard that it hath been said by them of old time . . . but I say unto you . . . ". It is difficult to imagine now the shock such language caused to Christ's contemporaries.

But perhaps the surest sign and most adequate proof of this quality of Christ's teaching is the steadfast refusal to argue or debate — Jesus declares, and so it is. His truth is, to the morally perceptive, quite self-evident. We may disregard His insights, we may deny His word, but it is we, and not the truth, that suffer in consequence. That is authority.

II

A second quality that distinguishes the teaching of our Lord is its *simplicity*. Whatever problems His words may raise, of faith or more often of obedience, we rarely are in doubt of what He means. Our difficulties — if we are honest — are not in understanding but in doing.

With what superb economy of words and dramatic force Jesus can tell a story to illustrate a truth or to implant a lesson! Equally effective are the epigrams that tease reflection into understanding: "A man's life is not in the abundance of the things that he possesses"; "New wine demands new wineskins"; "Sufficient for each day is its own ration of trouble!"; "Render unto Caesar the things which are Caesar's, and unto God the things which are God's".

Similar in purpose are the innumerable questions Jesus poses. Of the relation of outward conduct to inward character, He asks, "Do men gather grapes of thorns, or figs of thistles?" On anxiety: "Which of you, if you do take thought, can add a foot to his height?" Of the loss of spiritual integrity: "If the salt itself have lost its savour, wherewith shall it be salted?" On moral versus legal scruples — an inflammable issue — "Is it lawful to do good on the sabbath day, or to do evil?" And on ambition: "What is a man profited if he gain the whole world and lose his own soul?" This "Socratic" method of instruction, eliciting admissions from the taught, is deeply significant in its hidden implications.

Prosaic Western minds are often unaware of the subtle power of Jesus' poetry.

Consider the lilies of the field, how they grow:
They toil not
Neither do they spin,
Yet I tell you that even Solomon in all his glory
Was not arrayed like one of these.

Therefore be not anxious, saying
What shall we eat?
What shall we drink?
What shall we wear?
The gentiles seek all these things!
And your heavenly Father knoweth your need of them.
Seek first his kingdom,
And his righteousness,
And all these things shall be added as well.

Enter by the narrow gate:
For the gate is wide
And the way is easy
That leads to destruction:
And many are those who enter thereby!
But the gate is narrow,
And the way hard
That leads to life:
And few are those who find it!

Examples of such rhythmic patterns are innumerable, and once read with concentration, are not easily forgotten. Who that has once heard attentively —

Ask, and it will be given you,
Seek, and you will find,
Knock, and it will be opened unto you:
Everyone who asks, receives;
Everyone who seeks, shall find;
And to everyone who knocks, it shall be opened ...

ever completely forgets it afterwards?

Little wonder that the common people flocked to listen to teaching so memorable, so persuasive, and so true.

Did ever man speak thus? Was ever creature
In such language courted? When the heat
Of wilful madness wrought the soul's defeature,
The God that might have punished doth intreat!

Yet the winsome simplicity can mislead. The concrete imagery of the East, the challenging exaggeration of statement that provokes discussion, cannot always be accepted at face value. Such words as "If any have no sword, let him sell his shirt and buy one!", *cannot* be meant literally, any more than "I am the door", or "If thy hand offend thee, cut it off!" An excellent rule is: Be careful if you understand Christ's sayings literally; take the greatest pains to hear His words exactly; always take His utterances seriously, for they are life.

III

The least appreciated quality of Jesus' teaching is *reality*. No attitude to His message is so entirely ignorant or stupid as that which assumes it is impractical, unrealistic, irrelevant to the world we know. Jesus saw men and life with unblinking eyes, and described them candidly, sometimes almost ruthlessly.

A procession of unlovely people marches through Christ's sayings, each vividly portrayed because truthfully observed. A churlish neighbour refuses bread, a money-making farmer has no thought above his barns, an unfeeling glutton ignores the hungry at his door, a foolhardy youth, impatient of restraint, deserts his home. An unjust judge betrays his high responsibility, a rascal steward falsifies accounts, a lazy servant buries his lord's investment. The ruthless money-lender forecloses on a widow's mortgage. An envious farmer sows tares in a neighbour's crop.

As to religion, the ostentatious Pharisee makes piety mere window-dressing, and the flattery-loving scribe delights in titles; insincere disciples cry, "Lord, Lord", and disobey. The heartless priest ignores the injured traveller; the indifferent Levite passes on the other side.

The crafty politician — that fox Herod — the cunning litigant, the merciless debtor, the Roman press gang, carousing employees and domineering foremen, slave-driving overlords and tyrant rulers are all described. A fearful threat is uttered against the evil-minded blackguard with whom no children can be trusted. Here surely is no sentimentalist concerning people!

Nor does Jesus hide the harsh impartiality of life. The same fierce weather beats on the wise man's house as on the fool's; the tower falls, injustice is done, irrespective of personal merit. Good sowing may bring variable harvests, even in God's fields. Laws governing marriage are a necessary safeguard against men's heartlessness.

"From within, out of the heart of man, proceed evil thoughts, adulteries, fornication, murders, thefts, covetousness, wickedness, deceit, lasciviousness, ill-will, blasphemy, pride, foolishness: these defile the man!" Is this a want of realism? Far more reasonable might it be to charge Jesus with pessimism, or even cynicism, than with wishful and impractical idealism. But the moral heroism Jesus demands, and the optimism underlying all His strictures, sufficiently dispel such charges. Men are no angels, and life is no rosy dream; but much can be done about it, and it is still His Father's world.

IV

The themes of Jesus' teaching are intellectually bold and ethically bracing. He discourses of God, the Kingly Father, whose character is ever watchful love, whose reign brings infinite enrichment. He talks of life within the Father's family, of brotherliness, sympathy, forgivingness, and love. He opens up endless possibilities of the power of prayer and the victories of faith. He calls to service which is practical, uncalculating, freely given as need alone requires, without inducement or reward.

Jesus values the soul above all else — wealth, institutions, rituals, or ambitions. Life itself He sees against the background of eternity, and by this timeless dimension He condemns mere worldliness, evaluates character as infinitely worthwhile, comforts suffering, and warns against the immeasurable consequences of evil.

God and His unwearying love, man and his infinite value, love in its dedication to human need, life and its immortal hope — these are Christ's ruling thoughts; peace, humility, forgivingness, joy, and faith — these are His personal ideals. Within the circle of such thoughts and aims, all that He touches is illumined, every listening heart is searched, every conscience challenged, every burdened, weary soul is comforted. Never indeed spake any man like this Man.

V

Finally, and significantly, the appeal of Jesus' teaching is always to an innate knowledge of the truth, to the inner discernment that "can read the face of the sky and the portents of the seasons", the moral sense of ordinary folk. Conscience echoes to His truth. Hence His reiterated questions, His constant appeal in the parables and elsewhere to what men themselves would do. Hence, too, the searching challenge: "Why judge ye not, even of yourselves, that which is right?"

Why not indeed! To whom else can we go? This Man has words of eternal life.

14 Truth in a Tale

"He spake many things unto them in parables."

Matthew 13:3

EVERY SCHOOLBOY KNOWS that Jesus taught by illustrative stories and arresting metaphors. But not everyone realises just how typical of Jesus the parables are.

Here is the Master-thinker condescending to the mental limitations of a non-literary people, couching great ideas in attractive, memorable forms.

Here is the divine Teacher expressing spiritual truth and moral ideals in terms of concrete common life, impatient of the abstract generalities that so often baffle faith and cloud the conscience.

Here, too, is a technique of teaching which provokes the recognition of a truth by the listener's own thought-processes. "What think ye . . . ? What man of you . . . ?" What we think we saw for ourselves is much easier to believe than things we know we had to learn from others!

Though Jesus did not invent the parable — Aesop and the rabbis knew their value long before — Jesus used it as none other has done to write large enduring ideas on the imagination of the world. And what a treasury of thought the parables contain! No rapid summary can do justice to their wealth of meaning, but to see them as a whole illumines their method and crystallises their message.

I

Among the *parables of the Kingdom* are those of the pearl, the treasure, and several about feasting, whose purpose is to advertise the attractions and advantages of life under God's rule.

Others, of the sower, the seed growing secretly, the mustard seed, the leaven, concern the way the Kingdom comes, growing (or spreading) gradually by the slow extension of God's rule, through society and through the individual life, from the surrendered citadel of the heart outward to the frontiers of life's experience. The Kingdom does not evolve from

81

human idealism and endeavour: seed or leaven is inserted from without, and from above, a germ of divine life without which the human situation must remain inert soil, heavy, lifeless dough.

Each of these parables, too, implies that the process is hidden: the seed within the soil, the leaven in the dough. "It groweth up he knoweth not how." In that word is both warning against impatience, and encouragement against despair. Nevertheless, the result is sure: the whole will be leavened, the seed springs of itself, the tiny grain becomes a sheltering tree. In all these pictures of the advancing purposes of God there breathes a calm, unhurried confidence in the final rule of right.

The Kingdom depends nevertheless on human co-operation, and the parables point also to man's unreadiness and self-will as the twin obstacles to be overcome. The story of refused invitations to a royal wedding illustrates the strange reluctance of foolish men to accept God's beneficent and satisfying rule. Yet God *will* furnish the feast with guests, if necessary from the highways and the hedges. Even the bridesmaids who by privilege and preparation should be readiest of all (like the Jews in Jesus' day) are half unready when the moment comes. From the soil of numerous hearts the word of the Kingdom is snatched away, or choked with preoccupations, or starved by shallow natures.

God's reaction to man's unreadiness in all these parables of the Kingdom is withdrawal of the invitation. Opportunity comes suddenly to every soul; rejection may be final, but the resulting loss is always self-imposed.

II

Another group of Jesus' stories concerns *man's service of the ideal* in the promotion of God's rule in the affairs of life. In both versions of the parable of the talents, differences of natural endowment and of circumstantial opportunity are shown to be unimportant in assessing one's personal contribution to the work of God — reward is given to faithfulness rather than achievement. Equal faithfulness is possible to very unequal souls!

The story of the skilful scoundrel who trifled with his lord's accounts to cover up his defalcations has ever puzzled pious readers, until the essential point is sifted out. The rascal succeeds by a daring, a foresight, a practical good sense, which even his defrauded employer reluctantly admires. If, argues Jesus, ends so unworthy evoke such diligence and wit, why are the servants of the ideal so often slothful, dull, and uninspired?

Yet, as always with Jesus, the motive is all-important. The inexhaustible tale of the good Samaritan emphasises simple, genuine, unlimited because unconditional, compassion as the only sufficient reason for doing God's work among needy men.

The story of the labourers, who receive each his agreed reward at the absolute discretion of the Master, underlines again that it is a privilege, and not a right, to serve within the Kingdom. Where none is fit to serve, none can cavil at conditions or reward — all is of grace alone. We are, at our utmost best, unprofitable servants, more needing to be served than serving.

III

This thought of grace is fundamental to Christ's teaching; the Kingdom is a realm of saved, forgiven hearts.

Two sons, one promising but disobedient, the other defiant but finally obeying, and again two men praying in the Temple, one proudly rejecting mercy, the other penitently seeking it, illustrate the difference between the hostile Pharisees and the converted "sinful" who find salvation. And the further story of two debtors, one forgiven much, the other little, revealed with piercing clarity the motive which Jesus believed would nourish endless devotion and Christian effort — the motive of love awakened by forgiveness.

One other parable declares how the basis of the Kingdom in such love becomes the controlling principle of personal relationships. A servant mercifully released from an enormous debt exacts payment, threatening punishment, from a fellow servant owing a trivial amount. With unwonted sharpness Jesus affirms that the former cancellation was revoked, the utmost penalty imposed. For whoso will not forgive shall never find forgiveness.

But of all these *parables of salvation,* the most famous and most beautiful are the tales of the lost sheep, the lost coin, and the lost son. When His own attitude to sinful men was called in question, Jesus compared Himself to a shepherd, favourite Old Testament figure for God. The shepherd's responsibility, the shepherd's personal interests, the shepherd's heart — all demand recovery of the sheep lost from the flock, not for sentiment's sake, but for its value. Hence the relief and joy when the lost is safe again.

The diligent search by an anxious housewife for the missing heirloom, part of a wedding ornament of coins, is nothing to the tireless zeal of God's seeking out the sinner, and the joy of finding is re-echoed in heaven.

Nearer still to common human feeling, the lost son, whose absence, though wilful, brings grief and heartbreak to a sorrowing home, is relentlessly described in all his shame and lonely misery. His slow repentance, return, and welcome awaken sympathy and joy in every heart except a Pharisaic elder brother, jealous of a sinful man's salvation. Again love rejoices that the lost is found, and that is explanation in itself.

Each of these stories is a mine of evangelical suggestion, but the essential point is simple. By whatsoever means men become lost, God values them and loves them, and seeks their safe return. Heaven and earth rejoice together over one sinner that repenteth.

And that is Christ's explanation of Himself.

IV

As man can only enter the Kingdom by forgiveness, and only serve therein through grace, so he finds his inner resources sufficient only by means of prayer.

The power of persistent prayer is made memorable by two unexpected stories. One tells of a man confronting the hunger of travelling friends and needing to disturb an unwilling neighbour with clamorous pleadings for bread — his begging succeeds because it is sustained. The other concerns a widow seeking justice from a lazy, unscrupled judge, and forcing him at last to yield by her reiterated demands.

God is neither a grudging, impatient neighbour, nor an idle, unprincipled judge. The comparison lies in violent contrast. If even such a neighbour, even such a judge, may be prevailed upon at last by sheer persistence, how much more will a faithful, loving Father grant the requests whose sincerity has been sifted by time and delay!

"Men ought always to pray, and not to faint."

V

Of the final group, the sombre parables of the End, two things immediately command attention. Judgement is certain. A farmer hears the sentence on his fancied evident success: "This night thy soul shall be required of thee!" The rich glutton learns that "a great gulf is fixed". The word goes forth concerning the barren tree: "Cut it down"; the goats on the left hand of the judgement seat hear the solemn verdict: "Depart from me". The fate of the vineyard whose fruit has been withheld is forcibly described; the husbandmen are slain, the vineyard given to "others".

Though, as with the tares, the sifting may be long delayed, it yet must come. The fundamental distinction between right and wrong will be *eternally* affirmed, and that is judgement.

But what is judged? In every case the sin is an omitted good. The farmer is not rich toward God; the wealthy did not feed the beggar at his gate; the tree bore no fruit; the "goats" did not tend the needy; the husbandmen did not yield the Lord His increase. Not one accusation concerns positive, fleshly, passionate sin, the kind by us condemned. Not to do the good we can do, the good we ought to do, the good that He Himself has ever done for us — that in Christ's eyes merits final condemnation.

He who understands the parables understands the Christ. Not the whole circle of Christian truth can be found within their frame, but all that is essential to practical discipleship is illustrated here: the nature of the Kingdom and its coming to the heart; its laws of service, diligence, and love; the meaning and necessity of grace, God's answer to man's sin; the need of prayer; and certainty of final judgement on the misused life. And through them all there breathes the unmistakable assurance that in Himself and in His word men, if they choose, can find salvation.

"He that hath ears to hear, let him hear!"

15 Character Immaculate

"I have given you an example."　　　　　　　　John 13:15

As THE PORTRAIT of Jesus has been the dream and the despair of artists in every generation, so His peerless character has been the delight and the defeat of many pens. Sometimes the figure of the human Master cannot be seen through the mists of pious awe. Sometimes the preoccupations of the age distort the picture. Men of a hard relentless time will dwell upon the Christ of otherworldly hopes and compensations. Men of an ugly, ruthless time will see Christ as the charming Hero of the "Galilean idyll". A frightened, war-torn world will see a pacifist Christ, mild and always inoffensive.

Sometimes, too, aesthetic traditions of church-decoration have concentrated the attention of generations of worshippers upon the effeminate, too-good-for-this-world, stained-glass figures of Jesus that adorned the medieval churches. Without doubt, and probably without exception, men see in Jesus some reflection of their own time and thought, experience and ideals.

To get behind tradition, prejudice, and the projection of one's own assumptions demands a constant discipline of imagination by the written record of His life and words. Even so, much depends for the final portrait on what is assumed to be the foundation quality of Christ's character, the point of view from which all facets of His human personality may be seen in their consistency.

In our day, in view of the over-emphasis of the past and the problems that beset our age, the character of Jesus can best be understood if we see all other qualities in relation to His quite astonishing *strength*. What one long ago described as Jesus' "robust manliness and steel-tempered will-power", was the centre from which His personality radiated and in which His character found its harmony.

I

We are not here immediately concerned with the physical strength that could endure the crowded days and sleepless nights, the ceaseless journeys and the final intense concentration of bodily suffering. Nor need we elaborate the strength of mind expressed in the utter realism of His outlook, the unflinching courage of His passion. These forms of personal power stem from that strength of character which made Him first the Leader, then the Hero, Master, and Lord of strong, essentially masculine disciples; and which — no less certainly — made it impossible for enemies to ignore Him or despise Him. They could not but oppose His forcefulness with whatever weapons lay to hand.

Glimpses of this innate strength of soul are given us in the strange scene at Nazareth, where all desired to throw Him from the cliff, but no one dared lay hands on Him; in His effective dispersal, single-handed, of an excited crowd intent on forcefully asserting His kingship; in His face "set as a flint" to go to Jerusalem.

We see it in His unopposed "cleansing" of the Temple, in His complete self-mastery at His arrest, in His strong silence before Herod, the calm dignity that outraged Caiaphas, the personal ascendancy that exasperated Pilate.

One feels the same strength behind Christ's searching criticism of authorities, institutions, ideas, individuals, and — much more dangerous — of ancient sacred traditions. One feels it in His anger at callousness, hypocrisy, or cruelty.

One senses Christ's strength in His resolute refusal to abate His terms of discipleship, despite His deep desire that men might follow and be saved. And it was the moral strength of Jesus, expressed in His aggressive programme of attack, appeal, and warning, especially in the last week of mounting challenge, which finally forced the hands of the political and religious leaders and compelled the nation to decide about His claims.

Unsparing realism of outlook, unyielding firmness of purpose, uncompromising assertion of truth, unflinching acceptance of pain, unhesitating adherence to duty, and implacable demand for decision add up to a character that *must* be reckoned with, deferred to, or destroyed.

II

Such force of character disciplined by mercy and unselfishness is gentleness. Tenderness bereft of strength is merely softness, weakening in its effect on others and undermining in its reaction on oneself. The compassion of Christ derives not merely from a ready sympathy but from deep anger against heartlessness, and strong indignation against so much of suffering in His Father's world. Christ's is emphatically a strong gentleness.

It is shown in a hundred moving ways. Lepers too long isolated from all friendly companionship, thrilled to His touch — at once caress, compassion, command, and also defiance of prevailing social and religious taboos. Jesus understands acutely the dependence of the blind upon the tones of voice addressed to them; He enters swiftly into the feelings of the poor, the bereaved and lonely, the criticised and helpless.

He singles out for strong encouragement the shrinking soul within the crowd, receives with ready kindliness the infants brought to Him for blessing, foresees the difficulties of a young girl raised from death, and with exquisite insight enables the brokenhearted Peter to retrace His steps.

No one had reason to fear the strength of Jesus, except as they might fear the judgement of God. All His forcefulness sprang to defend the sad, the oppressed, the meek, the friendless, and the penitent. For all such His tenderness was mighty, His very pity was omnipotent.

III

As the discipline of gentleness ensured that the strength of Christ could never hurt, so the dedication of tireless goodwill laid all His powers and grace, in positive and costly ways, entirely at the service of His fellows. This we usually term "love", but the word is totally inadequate. The steadfast, unlimited, unconditioned goodwill of Christ was not primarily emotional; it was never mere impulsive charity; it had nothing whatever about it of sentimental muddleheadedness.

Shallow compliments, unconsidered encouragement, flattering misjudgement, unthinking optimism, were never on His lips, nor were mere expressions of well-wishing, unmatched by effort. His "love" was essentially practical, relevant, spontaneous, un-self-seeking. Whereas the Stoic "loved mankind", Jesus did good to men; whereas many have spoken vaguely and abstractly of the "other-regarding sentiment", Jesus washed men's feet, tended their suffering, comforted their sorrow, was forgiving to His enemies, died to save those who had betrayed Him.

Thus out of His fulness many received, and all who sought His help found Him inexhaustible. None came in vain, none needed to come twice, and none had to justify his coming or argue his desert. "Love" in Jesus was the spontaneously outflowing goodwill of a nature inherently sympathetic, morally free of self-concern, mentally quick to perceive another's inner need, and spiritually endowed with rich resources to make goodwill not an emotional indulgence in hand-wringing pity but an energetic enterprise in doing good.

IV

It is in the light of His immense personal force that the purity of Jesus also is to be understood. His strength is not only disciplined into gentleness and dedicated into love, it was triumphantly resistant to every approach of evil. In Christ, purity rises from a negative virtue to a positive and powerful sanctity of mind, feeling, and will, equally evident in everything He said, did, permitted, or suffered.

The holiness of Jesus was something additional to His sinlessness. It was experienced rather as a subduing, heartbreaking, soul-cleansing power that searched the dark places of the soul and brought confession unbidden to the lips. So Peter at the lakeside, bitterly aware of his dire need that Christ take charge of his life as well as of his boat, blurts out, "Depart from me, for I am a sinful man, O Lord!" So Zaccheus, convicted, protests publicly his conversion to the way of righteousness and restitution; the woman of Samaria finds in Christ One "who told me all things whatsoever I did"; and the woman taken in adultery remains to face things out with Jesus when others less willing for His searching slink cowardly away.

Christ's depth of purity made it possible for His companions later to worship Him as Lord; and already, before the resurrection, the purging influence of His personal presence exposed, convicted, purified, and renewed wherever a sinful soul consented to be saved.

This antiseptic quality of moral insight and truth, of something inexorably straight and clean, in whose presence the false and shameful could not live, must ever be remembered when the greatness of Christ's claims, and the devotion which He asked and men gave, are being weighed. Unquestionably it was this quality more than any other that enshrined Christ's power to transform sinful men and made credible the suggestion that He was indeed divine, the only-begotten Son of the everlasting God.

V

Thus enemies, friends, suppliants, penitents, and observers unite in testimony to the forceful character of Jesus, source of His human power, His gentleness, His inexhaustible love and unassailable purity. The inner secrets of such all-enabling strength are not obscure or magical. His entire personality was unified, centred upon one, single, undeviating purpose. Where in us division of mind inevitably weakens, in Him concentration multiplied strength. He lived under an unslackening sense of spiritual compulsion: "I must" is His watchword, "This commandment I received . . . " His only self-justification. And He lived from a great depth of being: "I live by the Father . . . . My Father is with me".

Such concentration, motived by consecration, nourished by communion, reinforced His life with superhuman powers, enabling Him — strong Son of God — to save to the uttermost all that come unto God by Him.

CRISIS THAT FOREBODES REJECTION

Contention: *the Stranger of Galilee*
Conflict: *the seeds of strife*
Crisis: *"Who am I?"*
Confirmation: *Christ transfigured*
Counter-attack: *on to the offensive!*

16 Contention: The Stranger of Galilee

"Art thou only a stranger?"   Luke 24:18

"HE SHALL GROW UP before him as a root out of dry ground. He hath no form nor comeliness, and when we shall see him there is no beauty, that we should desire him." So warned the prophet, and so it was.

> He came from His blest throne
> Salvation to bestow,
> But men made strange, and none
> The longed-for Christ would know. . . .

At Bethlehem they turned Him from the inn; in Galilee He sometimes had not where to lay His head; in Samaria the villages refused to entertain Him; at Jerusalem His own received Him not. Even of the twelve He could ask, "Have I been so long time with you, and yet hast thou not known me?" Still on Easter morning Mary could mistake Him for the gardener.

This is the saddest irony of history, that He who came farthest to meet with us, stepping down from glory to walk with men their homeward journey to an evening rest, should walk unknown, unrecognised, and, far too frequently, unwelcome.

"Art thou only a stranger?" Too often yet the answer has to be, Yes, only a stranger. An altar stood in Athens to the Unknown God: a cross was raised at Calvary for the unknown Christ.

I

Failure to recognise Jesus was not due simply to spiritual blindness. Much about Him was strange. He did not fall neatly into pre-arranged categories, within plain definitions.

His thought was strange: in a day of militant political nationalism He pointed to another Kingdom, whose ways were ways of pleasantness, and all her paths were peace. In a nation convinced that material prosperity was the proof and evidence of divine blessing, Jesus called men to renounce all, take up a cross, and follow Him to ruin. In a Roman world which worshipped force, He preached a self-effacing gentleness that turned the other cheek in meekness and goodwill.

All human ideas and values were reversed in His kind of world. He declared those blessed whom the world profoundly pitied, those triumphant whom the world considered beaten. It is not strange men found Him hard to comprehend.

His life was strange: renouncing all the insignia of power, He lived simply and with utter self-effacement. His associates were society's castaways, His methods politically ineffectual, His constituency the handicapped, despised, and negligible. He was a Messiah of no known or expected brand, strangely out of tune with all His generation hoped.

His claims were strange: unlike the prophets, He seemed often to speak in His own name. He declared forgiveness, revised freely the accepted law, so spake that disease, possession, affliction, even death, gave way to Him. He invited men to find salvation in Himself, claimed their faith, and commanded their obedience.

He spake often of the Father as one with Himself; of Himself as Son in some unique fashion to the Father. He assumed a past in glory with the Father, a future in glory in His Kingdom, and attributed to Himself the supreme function of universal judgement. In Himself — He taught — God moved among men, and had become visible. In dealing with Him men dealt with God, and so decided their eternal destinies.

All this were easy to dismiss if He Himself were not profoundly strange, indeed unique, in character, spirit, authority, power, and influence. None could convict Him of self-seeking, of megalomania, or of delusion. He was humble, unassuming, devoted to the service of the lowest folk, a kindly Teacher with a fund of stories and a train of maladjusted, dependent people of the common sort!

Hearing Him, men were aware of divine illumination; watching Him, men were moved as by divine compassion. His very piety was strange, for no confession, plea for pardon, or prayer for deeper consecration issued from His lips. Men knew that He was sinless, and heard Him speak always from an unbroken sense of filial perfection.

And His end was strange: He passed into the hands of wicked, time-serving officials, betrayed, forsaken, rejected, crucified. And so He died, a painful, lonely, shameful death upon a felon's stake amid a jeering crowd.

Strangest of all, men said, and multitudes believed, that Jesus rose again.

No estimate of Jesus, and certainly no proffered "explanation" of the story, deserves to be taken seriously which does not full justice to this irreducible element of the odd, the despair of all neat definitions and facile theories, in the portrait of our Lord.

II

Is it so surprising that men felt baffled in His presence? At Nazareth they asked: "Is not this the carpenter?" Herod set on foot through Galilee enquiries concerning who He was. At Capernaum the people wondered, at Bethany they argued, on the open sea they whispered, "What manner of man is this?" Ever there clung about Him that which made men stop and stare. Men found Him hard to label, harder still to classify, explain, or yet ignore. He just did not "belong".

And this is deeply, permanently important. It is not very long since clever minds thought they had accounted for Jesus in humanistic terms. The disciples, we were told, upon a noble impulse, had invented the glorious portrait and the tale in accordance with their own exalted faith. The Jesus of the Gospels is the projection backwards of the hopes, the dreams, the messianic idealism of His age. Jesus did not create the Church, the Church created Jesus, or at least so far refashioned the story in the light of current dogma and ecstatic expectation as to hide the real Jesus forever from our eyes.

It was a futile theory, anyway. It left the real question — the source of such sublime faith and inspiration — still unanswered. And it created three or four others equally inexplicable.

But the theory of a myth-creating faith that constructed Christ out of odds and ends of contemporary hopes and superstitions, popular expectations and messianic dogma, founders fatally on the strangeness of the portrait that re-

95

sulted. So far from satisfying or fulfilling the longings of His generation, He outraged them. So far from being the creation of faith, the Jesus of the Gospels was faith's greatest stumbling block — to Jew and Greek alike.

A Messiah of the common people, a carpenter, at Nazareth of all places; tempted of the devil, rejecting a throne to teach and heal; befriending outcasts, consorting with the sinful, denying every cherished hope and privilege of Israel! He challenged her traditions, criticised her leaders, warned the chosen people of coming doom and envisaged the salvation of the Gentiles. Disowned by sects and synagogue, opposed by Pharisees and priests, rejected in the end even by the crowd, and forsaken at the last by His few friends — what Messiah is this? Not *thus* would Jewry, or any inexplicable first-century band of spiritual geniuses, fired with a passion for their own martyrdom, have "projected" Jesus. To the end He puzzled and offended friends and foes alike. He remained, except to faith, a Stranger, "out of this world".

III

And the strangeness abides about Him still. Familiar caricatures of Jesus, the half-angel, half-woman of the children's books, the idealistic Dreamer, the social Reformer with a passion for the underprivileged, the sorry Victim of adverse social pressures, are all distorted glimpses of His glory, due largely to unwillingness to let Him be Himself. We have so often lost the Figure in the phrases, wrapped up the truth of His enigmatic person in philosophies and creeds until we have forgotten what He is really like. The modern Church in fact needs nothing more desperately than a fresh introduction to her Lord, a new discipline in the four Gospels.

For we have all tried to *humanise* the Stranger, bring Him within our comprehension, reduce Him to our terms, until we have almost lost Him. Jesus was most certainly not the founder of a worldly welfare state where cushioned security may lull the conscience and breed selfishness. Nor was He the herald of a "spiritual" message about some distant future glory without relevance for earth and time. He came to this world, and for this world — but from another, and intent upon making another sort of world out of the mess of this, another sort of people out of the people we are. He belongs in a different dimension, and demands we follow Him "in step with a distant drum", to ends beyond all ordinary conceiving, in obedience absolute and final. He speaks to us as God — and shames our little faith.

IV

Still more does the world need to see the Stranger as He was. Above the mists of scepticism, the slanders of His enemies, the failures of His Church, has ever shone the commanding figure of the Christ. The unbelieving world has always been ready to abuse the Church, quibble about the Bible, challenge the Christian tradition, criticise the prevalent Christian ethic, but before the greatness of the Master antagonism hesitates. The beauty of His story, the finality of His teaching, the perfection of His character, the challenge of His claims, the achievements of His power make men pause and wonder.

And where men wonder, faith is possible. He is not content to remain a Stranger. He calls His witnesses, and He sends His Spirit, to make Himself known. He comes Himself, to walk beside us till we beg Him stay, and then our eyes are opened. Whenever we are willing, we can know just who the Stranger is. As one among the very greatest of His modern followers has said, "To those who obey Him, whether they be wise or simple, He will reveal Himself, in the toils, the conflicts, the sufferings which they shall pass through in His fellowship, till as an ineffable mystery they shall learn in their own experience *who He is*."

17 Conflict: The Seeds of Strife

"And they were offended at him."   Mark 6:3

HOW COULD ANYONE consider Christ offensive? Our own generation finds Him hard to understand, and so ignores Him. Some generations have found Him so unwelcome as fiercely to deny Him. His own generation found Him so offensive as to put Him violently to death. But long before that ultimate madness, the currents had set in against Him, and the shadows of the fatal storm had gathered around His head.

Hardly has Mark's story of the Master got under way when the tide of opposition rises, wave upon wave. "Who is this that forgives sins? . . . He eateth with publicans and sinners! . . . Why do thy disciples fast not? . . . Why do they on the sabbath day that which is not lawful? . . . They watched whether he would heal on the sabbath day, that they might accuse him . . . . By the prince of the devils he casteth out devils! . . . He hath an unclean spirit . . . . Is not this the carpenter? . . . When they saw his disciples eat bread with unwashen hands they found fault . . . . They were offended at him."

How should such a Christ offend?

The true answer is illuminating. As Jesus Himself expressed it when explaining to the disciples the dwindling of of the Galilean crowds, the varying harvest reveals the differing soils in which the seed of truth is sown. Some are shallow, covering only thinly the underlying rock, thus yielding a quick show of growth that soon withers in the heat. Wayside soil is trodden hard by passing feet, and into it the seed never really enters. Beneath the hedgerows and in untilled corners the soil is filled already with the seeds of thistle and thorn whose strong profusion chokes the good seed's growth. Even the harvest of the good soil varies: "some thirtyfold, some sixtyfold, some an hundred".

Here is the authoritative diagnosis of the frustrations that beset all Christian enterprise.

I

Christ's early months in Galilee were filled with crowds.
Men could not get at Him for the press: thousands waited
on His word. The seed sprang up. Then many "walked no
more with Him". Having no root, they withered. Jesus
refused the crown which they so gladly would have won
for Him, when He fed them free within the wilderness; and
the refusal hurt. Earth hath no malice like popular expectation disillusioned by the truth.

So long as the common folk thought Christ's lowly mien
and winsome methods were but disguise, excitement ran
high. But they tired of waiting for the manifestation of
His real power in armed revolt. They tired of preaching,
of the call to repentance, of the moral lessons on love and
obedience. To the end there were those whose partisanship
protected Him from open assualt, but Jesus was at once too
lowly and too spiritual to arouse the crowd's enthusiasm —
they followed only until they saw His meaning, then drifted
away.

Some earnest folk cherished the hope that when Messiah
had made Israel great, spiritual revival and religious reform
would follow. But even these, when they saw Jesus reverse
the order, became impatient of His methods and contemptuous of His aim, saying in effect, "We will not have this man
to reign over us". So, in the final days, the Jewish crowd
lent their voices to ingratitude's basest cry: "Crucify him!"

He is a strong man who knowingly, willingly rejects the
allurements of popularity to maintain the truth. Christianity
has not always resisted the temptation to woo shallowly
the shallow crowd. "Jesus . . . saw much people, and was
moved with compassion toward them, because they were as
sheep not having a shepherd." It will be a sad day when that
deep compassion over people dies out of the Church. But
compassion must not conceal the truth; repentance and
obedience alone can lead to life. Discipleship begun without
that realisation must wither and die. And if the crowd will
not believe, they must be allowed to turn away.

II

Few things are so impervious to truth as prejudice fortified
by dogmatism and encased in religious pride! By devious

and sad processes of spiritual decay, the once invaluable sect of Pharisees, guardians of evangelical ideals and pious hope, had become in Jesus' day the representatives of a religious assurance and self-righteousness which nothing could impress. Confident of every divine favour, entrenched in Jewish law and tradition, toughened by long persecution, and now the accepted spiritual leaders of the chosen people, the Pharisees acknowledged no authority but their own, tolerated no religious teaching but their doctrines, and enforced with every possible sanction whatever distinguished the "good Jew" from the rest of men.

No one is so fiercely opposed, or so bitterly slandered, as he who attacks bad religion in the name of good. Doubtless the Pharisees were jealous of Jesus' authority and influence with the common folk, but zeal for Judaism as they knew it inflamed their envy. By omitting the customary fasts, healing on the sabbath, making jest of ceremonial washings, befriending the outcasts and the irreligious, Jesus fatally offended the pious scruples of the stricter Jews.

When, in addition, He challenged the prevailing opinions about vows, meats, the meaning of righteousness, the interpretation of Scripture and the divine favour towards Israel, He earned the opprobrium of innovator, heretic, blasphemer. His reassertion in Israel of the living truth, spoken in contemporary terms and in the power of the Spirit, could find no welcome in minds which could not see the truth for written texts. Moreover, His damaging criticism of their self-righteousness, their ostentation, their want of sympathy and of redemptive concern, and their frequent hypocrisy added passion to their prejudice.

So it became morally impossible for Pharisees to measure Christ's work fairly or weigh His high claims justly. Self-assurance, self-righteousness, and self-defence together form an impenetrable shield against the darts of truth. The seed lies on the hardened surface of closed mind and calloused conscience, and can take no root. Christ has often to plough up the beaten soil of a man's religiousness in order to convert his soul.

III

Of the scribes (religious solicitors), priests, and politicians it may fairly be said that they had a vested interest in thistles, thorns, and brambles. Jesus constituted a very real threat to all their policies and position. The scribe could scarcely countenance the religious teaching of an unprofessional and untrained layman. The priests heard with dismay Christ's strictures upon the Temple worship and the ritual tithes, and were moved to deepest anger by His challenge to their Temple market.

The politicians, whether Sadducees anxious to maintain existing relationships with Rome, or Herodians pledged to preserve the alliance of the Herod family with Caesar, saw in any messianic movement an acute danger to their whole security. "If we let him alone, the Romans will come and take away our place . . . . "

Amid so many selfish, worldly interests to be preserved, where could the seeds of love and truth take root? In lives so cluttered with ambition, self-seeking, secular aims, and self-preservation the Kingdom could make no progress without far-reaching revolution — it would cost too much to clear the ground.

That is precisely where the challenge of Jesus finds us in the twentieth century. We could be well content to make of Christianity a stimulating hobby for our leisure time, a decoration and an enrichment of an already busy life, full of settled aims and well-established personal routines. It is the total claim of Christ that we resent — the danger of upheaval that we fear. For Jesus tolerates no rival claim, will share the soul with no prior interests. His rule collides in us with the cares of this world, the demand for security, and all the secular interests of our crowded days and overcrowded hearts. The seed is choked.

IV

It is idle to pretend that Christ does not thus threaten our shallow worldliness, confront our prejudices, and challenge our innumerable preoccupations. He demands now, as He did then, that men sit down and assess the cost of becoming His disciples. And sometimes still we find the cost too high.

Christ offers a kind of deliverance the modern world needs but does not want — a spiritual redemption through faith and love, obedience to the highest reforming society by regenerating men. He disturbs our favourite opinions, dwarfs our treasured ideals, revolutionises our comfortable judgements, makes our racial, social, intellectual, and religious prejudices look extremely silly. He exposes our false assumptions and would rebuild our lives according to new patterns — and we are afraid that we might lose too much!

So we oppose Him still. With two thousand years in which to learn that His way of living cannot be improved upon, that all other ways lead surely to disaster, that without His wisdom and His grace mankind is intellectually blind and morally bankrupt, we still distrust, deny or, what is worse, ignore Him.

When Jesus came to Birmingham they simply passed Him by,
They never hurt a hair of Him, they only let Him die;
For men had grown more tender, and they would not give
*   Him pain:*
They only just passed down the street and left Him in
*   the rain . . . .*
The crowds went home and left the streets without a soul
*   to see:*
And Jesus crouched against a wall and cried for Calvary.

Yet nothing is more certain in all human experience than that the soul opposed to Jesus is opposed to all its own best interests. The heart that finds Christ offensive is losing its power of moral discernment; the heart that is antagonistic is a heart bent upon its own final desolation.

18 Crisis: "Who am I?"

"Whom do men say that I am?"   Mark 8:27

OF THE FOUR POINTS between which the life of Jesus moves, Bethlehem, Jordan, Caesarea, and Calvary, Caesarea is certainly the least known, but it is by no means the least important. The beginning and the end are strictly unintelligible without this focal centre, the place of crucial questioning and irrevocable reply.

To this secluded spot among the foothills of Mount Hermon Jesus withdrew with the disciples, far from the pressing crowds and the endless strife of tongues, to face with them the great crisis of His ministry. Everything that had gone before — preaching, miracles, self-manifestation — had led up to this moment. Everything that followed, the challenge and the passion, hinged upon this event. Here Jesus reviewed the work that He had done and measured its results; here He announced the work He had yet to do, and defined its implications.

Before Caesarea, the keyword of the story had been *crowds;* afterwards, all is tuned from the bass note of the *cross.*

I

At Caesarea, a new and vital decision was asked of the disciples. Deliberately, even dramatically, Jesus provoked it by His questioning. In effect He asked them: "Well, how far have we got; what have we accomplished? What impression has My message and ministry made upon the people? Who are they saying that I am?"

It was not hard to answer. On every side men were saying things about Jesus, and saying great things. Some, impressed with His miraculous powers, thought He was John the Baptist risen from the dead. Some, impressed with His prophetic authority, were saying He was Elijah, returned to herald the Messiah. Some, remembering His tenderness, believed that He was Jeremiah, perhaps the greatest of all Israel's saints and heroes. Men were divided about Jesus, but they were discussing Him; and the majority were agreed that He stood among the very greatest of the men of God — a prophet, no less.

But exalted though that estimate of Jesus was, He was not satisfied. For one thing, the reply was insufficient. He knew Himself to be greater than any prophet, hero or saint. For another thing, the reply was secondhand, and Jesus ever required a personal response. "Whom do ye say that I am?" And Peter, impetuous and daring, voiced the long-pondered, slowly-won conviction of their hearts: "Thou art the Christ, the Son of the living God".

That was the point towards which Christ had worked for two years and a half. He had never yet claimed to be Messiah, for the term was capable of dangerous misunderstanding. He had waited for the truth to break by its own light upon the inner circle of disciples. Now it had come. What their confession meant to Jesus can be felt in His emotional outburst: "Blessed art thou, Simon bar-Jona, for flesh and blood hath not revealed it unto thee, but my Father". With these His chosen colleagues now convinced, Christ can go forward to challenge the whole nation, and accept the consequences.

In Peter's words, Jesus reads the promise of countless thousands who in coming generations would echo, with adoring gratitude, "Thou art the Christ, the King, Son of the living God, our Lord and our Redeemer".

It is significant that this great confession was first made at Caesarea. Here had stood for centuries a grotto sacred to the great god Pan, symbol of all that was lovely and sensual in pagan nature-worship. Here Philip had beautified the town, renaming it Caesarea in honour of Augustus. And here, supreme above the clamouring of the flesh and the claims of worldly power, Jesus is first by human lips acknowledged Lord, of nature and of men.

> *Pan, Pan is dead,*

and Caesar gone; but Christ abides, and of His Kingdom there shall be no end.

II

The disciples' new and vital decision was rewarded with a new and startling disclosure. *"From that time forth* began

Jesus to show unto his disciples how that he must go unto Jerusalem and suffer many things, and be killed, and be raised again the third day." For the first time, openly, He tells His disciples that the Messiah is not, as the crowds imagined and the scribes taught and they themselves dreamed, a glorious King clothed in majesty and riding to triumph amid the ruin of His foes. Messiah is first the Servant, establishing a reign of grateful love by reconciling sinful men through His death to the Kingly Father. Rebelliousness must be done away in love, distrust give place to faith; and for that removal of the inner obstacles to God's rule, Messiah's sacrificial death for man is unavoidable. The King must suffer, for the King is Saviour.

The disciples are aghast, and Peter promptly voices their indignant protest. This was the crowning offence of Jesus to Jewish minds — that Messiah should die. This is the crowning offence of Jesus to all minds — that Jesus should need to die, to deal with sin. That He should be wounded for our transgressions, bruised for our iniquities, leaves us so unpayably indebted to a totally undeserved atonement that human pride rebels. Yet so it is: the King must die that the Kingdom might come.

For the remaining six months of His ministry Jesus strove to prepare the disciples for the coming test of faith. He Himself set His face toward Jerusalem and marching in the freedom of a soul unconquered and unafraid, strode forward to the cross. But the disciples found it harder to adjust their thoughts, though the re-interpretation of Messiahship which Jesus had achieved in the wilderness temptation had in the end to become an integral part of their thinking, too.

And of ours. The towering barrier of man's self-will, disputing with his Maker for the crown of this poor world, must be scaled, and the faithless, wayward, foolish, self-assertive heart of man subdued by one great act of costly love, before the rule of God begins. We have not learned the deepest lesson about ourselves, our sin, our Saviour, until we have been with Him to Caesarea to discover, once for all, that there can be no Kingdom without the cross, no crown of glory without first a crown of thorns.

III

So vital a decision, so startling a disclosure, could not but involve a vast change in the meaning of discipleship. The new and challenging demand implied in such a re-interpretation of Messiahship was made unmistakably explicit: "If any man will come after me, let him deny himself, take up his cross, and follow me".

The twelve had stayed with Jesus from mixed motives — love, admiration, plain ambition. Even yet they will contend for places in His Kingdom. At Caesarea they learn there is to be no earthly kingdom, no enriching conquests; but a Kingdom reached by way of loss, rejection, and suffering. Its only weapon was, they learned, to be the truth, its only power love, its only greatness pre-eminence in service; its standard was the cross, and the path thereto lay through conflict, self-denial, and pain.

So serious a revaluation of discipleship took time. All hesitated; one refused. But eleven finally accepted, and to them Jesus committed His redeeming cause as He marched on to die.

There comes a time in every Christian life when the heart must adjust its thinking to accept the cross. We may follow at first intoxicated with the vision of a brave new world, a truth resolving all perplexity, allured by the charm and strength of Jesus, or the wondrous invitation to find in Him our peace. But soon or late there comes the challenge of the cross.

> Thou sayest, "Take up thy cross,
>   O man, and follow Me."
> The night is black, the feet are slack,
>   Yet would we follow Thee.

But all too often we modern Christians obey in some high moment of infectious zeal, and spend the rest of our days adjusting the cross more snugly to our shoulders, paring down its implications, inventing exceptions to our promises, and retracting our enthusiasm until in the end our self-will remains safely uncrucified!

IV

Complete discipleship involves following Jesus all the way — bowing before Him with awe at Bethlehem, standing with Him in dedication in the Jordan, sitting with Him for instruction at Caesarea, kneeling with Him in prayer within Gethsemane, being crucified with Him at Golgotha, and rising with Him on Easter day to newness of life. No step may be omitted, least of all the journey out to Caesarea to face the issues and clearly, firmly, once for all *decide* about the Stranger.

Jesus will be satisfied with nothing less than personal confession of His Lordship, personal commitment to His programme. Constantly He faced men with determinative questions about Himself: "Believest thou? . . . . Lovest thou me? . . . What think ye of Christ? . . . Whom say ye that I am?" The half-decided, He says in one scathing judgement, are unfit for the Kingdom.

So sooner or later He brings us all to Caesarea, to discover where He stands with us, and for us to decide what He means to us. To live under the influence of His teaching, surrounded by the sentiments of Christian culture, heirs to a Christian tradition and home, is not enough. All this must crystallise into personal faith in Christ: all further understanding, victory, service, peace wait on that decision.

And we must decide with all the implications clear before our minds, and with His solemn warning ringing in our ears: "He that is not with me, is against me!"

19 Confirmation: Christ Transfigured

"After six days . . . he was transfigured before them."
Mark 9:2

IT IS PROFITLESS to speculate upon what precisely happened on the Mount of Transfiguration. That the communion of Jesus with His Father should lend a new radiance to His spirit will surprise no one familiar with the power of prayer to re-kindle the inner fires of personality. But what more happened is not clear.

Each record stresses that Elijah and Moses, representing prophecy and law, and so signifying between them the sum of Old Testament revelation, "appeared" and talked with Jesus. Luke adds that their topic was the coming death of Jesus at Jerusalem.

Luke speaks of heavy sleep; both Mark and Luke suggest that the disciples were not in complete possession of their faculties; Matthew plainly calls the experience a "vision". Apostolic circles at any rate were certain that it was no trick of the setting sun; they represented Peter's testimony in the form: "We were eyewitnesses of his majesty . . . when we were with him in the holy mount." That is probably as much as we shall ever know.

Materialist or psychological explanations are less important, however, than what the experience signified, to Jesus, and to the three disciples; and what it signifies in consequence to us.

I

Jesus returned from the crucial discussions at Caesarea Philippi intent upon His final challenge to Jerusalem, well knowing what awaited Him. Before setting out, He retired to the solitude and peace of the high places, and here in the company of the closest three He sought in a season of prayer the clarity, the courage, and the calmness which His fateful journey would demand. It was a rehearsal, and a foretaste, of Gethsemane. And He was not disappointed.

As at His baptism, when Jesus faced His task in Galilee, the Father's voice assured Him of His Sonship and commission, so here on the mountain, as Jesus leaves Galilee to face the cross, the assurance is repeated. But now there is given in addition, and in strongest terms, the divine certainty that in Himself the high promise of His nation's past and preparation, the rigorous discipline of the law, the forward-pointing sacrificial system, and the gracious promise of the prophets are about to be fulfilled.

In one way these exceptional moments in the experience of Jesus only emphasise how closely He shared our burden and our need. He, too, was "heard in that he feared". In answer to prayer "all heaven came down His soul to greet", and to match Him for His fearful task. He could say to us that men ought always to pray and not to faint because He intimately knew its truth. The strength of purpose and unflinching courage which mark His last days in Judea find their source upon this hilltop in far Galilee. Jesus always won His battles in the secret place, before the issue had been joined, or the enemy was yet in sight!

II

What the Transfiguration meant for the disciples is revealed in the choice of only the trusted three to witness the event, and in the charge to silence afterwards. The experience provided evidence for Christ's claim to be Messiah. Any unguarded talk about it might well lead to premature messianic excitement and possible revolt. This — as we saw — is the testimony of Peter: "We have not followed cunningly devised fables . . . we were eyewitnesses . . . in the holy mount". What they thought, and dared believe, at Caesarea, they now know to be the truth.

"After six days . . . " — an important spiritual principle is enshrined in the simple note of time, clearly defining the position of experience in the development of discipleship. Caesarea Philippi had witnessed a courageous faith committing itself to almost incredible truth: Jesus the carpenter of Nazareth is the Christ of God. Six days later, in answer to that venture of faith, there comes divine assurance.

That is the law of spiritual understanding. Unshakable conviction, certainty, proof follow upon belief. Reason conducts to the edge of human knowledge; thence, at the prompting of testimony, conscience, and Scripture, faith takes its leap — and lands upon both feet of experience and conviction. "Said I not unto thee," Jesus reminds Mary, "that if thou wouldest believe thou shouldest see . . . ?" Again, "He that willeth to do . . . shall know." A man must act upon the truth he sees before the greater truth can dawn upon his soul.

To some earnest students of religion this is admittedly a stumbling block, a serious vexation of the mind. It seems at first sight so illogical, "unscientific": should not the evidence be provided before the verdict is demanded? Should not the Transfiguration precede Caesarea?

In answer, two things must be said. First, that religious truth is essentially moral, and all progress in moral understanding does in fact depend upon obedience to the light we have. It is quite certain that if the message, ministry, and character of Jesus had awakened in the three no answering insight and spiritual trust, then no vision of Christ's glory would accomplish any *moral* good in hearts so blind and unresponsive. Unless the heart be true, the conscience clear according to its present understanding, no further understanding can be given. We learn, in moral wisdom as in appreciation of beauty and even in comprehension of the truth, not by instruction only but by practice and obedience.

But, secondly, the same process lies at the very heart of science, and is itself the inmost meaning of creative art. A brilliant hypothesis is but the informed guess of the trained and conscientious scientist: it is compounded of experience, intuition, judgement, and partial understanding. Then follows the experiment, which tests the hypothesis and provides new evidence and, if successful, adds to the sum of human certainty.

So the vision of the artist remains a nebulous, intuitive, unproved possibility, in which the artist passionately believes, until action and achievement translate it into fact.

Doubtless these parallels are not complete, but the principle holds. All personal, living, practical truth — the kind of knowledge that cannot be expressed in formulae — must be apprehended not by the processes of logic alone, but by the total personality, heart, mind, conscience, and moral will, else it eludes our grasp. The outgoing of the heart in trust at Caesarea, responding eagerly to all it had already seen in Jesus, leads naturally to the positive understanding of the truth made radiant at the Transfiguration. At Caesarea

> *the steps of faith*
> *Fall on the seeming void:*

on the mountain height they

> *find*
> *The Rock beneath.*

III

The careful timing of the Transfiguration is significant in another way. Caesarea had confronted the disciples both with the truth about Jesus and with the challenge of the cross. Can we doubt that during the six days' interval this solemn warning had occupied their thoughts and sometimes dismayed their hearts? And would not the mountain vision of the greatness and the glory of the Master who commanded them be just the necessary inspiration for arduous days ahead?

Our direct need, like theirs, in this matter of carrying the cross is not to summon our spiritual reserves and step out bravely, nor to remind ourselves grimly of the terms of our discipleship: it is to climb the mount of prayer and see the Christ transfigured, and know again that He for whom we strive and suffer is infinitely worthy, deserving more, far more, than we can give of service, loyalty, and sacrifice.

And the duties of discipleship, no less than the dangers, necessitate this heartening inspiration. Raphael's great painting of the Transfiguration divides the canvas almost equally between the rapturous vision on the mountain and the violence and frustration in the valley. There nine disciples were confronted with a tortured epileptic boy, and could not heal him. Below, Raphael seems to say, all is argument, hostility, accusation, failure; above, all is light and majesty, power and glory.

Whether Raphael intended a criticism of the Church's frequent powerlessness, despite her great profession, or offered a reminder of her immeasurable and invincible resources if she would but lift her eyes to her transfigured Lord, is not quite clear. But this is certain: Christian disciples cannot remain, as Peter proposed to do, for ever on the mountain, cosily withdrawn from all life's harsher duties. *They must come down,* become involved in the problem-ridden, pain-racked world. Yet they will not be of saving use unless the vision of the Christ remains still clear within their hearts.

Above a dark, divided, hostile, and bedevilled world, above a troubled, disunited, and despondent Church, above all valleys of the soul's humiliation and defeat, the Christ has risen, radiant and glorious. In the plenitude of His grace and power He is the answer to every human problem, the Healer of each smitten heart, the unfailing resource of every Christian worker beset with exacting or frustrating tasks.

Look up, says Raphael. Look up, says Mark. "This is my beloved Son, hear him", says God. Above the valley is the vision, and above the tragedies of earth stands the transfigured Christ, hope of the world and earnest of the triumph that shall be.

20   Counter-attack: On to the Offensive!

"He steadfastly set his face to go to Jerusalem."

Luke 9:51

A CLOUD PASSES the sun, and the day is suddenly dull. The key changes, and the music falls to a solemn mood, a slower tempo. Lights are dimmed and the stage is shadowed as tragedy moves to its tense climax. Even so, as Jesus turns from Galilee towards Jerusalem, there enters the gospel story a sharpened foreboding, a heightened, fearful expectancy. His manner grows more sombre, His words more grave, His spirit heavy, as the journey proceeds. Already the cross casts its baleful shadow down the long white road and draws towards their destiny the Master and His men.

I

Such is the atmosphere caught by the passing phrases, the astonishingly vivid cameos, of the gospel narrative. "It came to pass, when the time was come that he should be received up, he steadfastly [resolutely, with fixed purpose] set his face to go to Jerusalem." The unusual intentness and resolution in His bearing left this memory for Luke long afterwards to recapture.

Mark recalls the same solemn moment: "They were in the way going up to Jerusalem; and Jesus was moving on before them: and they began to wonder; and as they followed him, they began to be afraid." How lifelike that is! Fixed purpose wraps Him in deep thought, His pace quickens until He is striding on ahead; they become aware of another distance between themselves and Him, a distance of understanding. With bewilderment comes foreboding, sharpening into fear. So Peter remembered, and described it all to Mark.

Luke continues with a constant sense of purposeful movement, almost of haste: "His face was as though he would go to Jerusalem . . . as they went in the way . . . as they went . . . He went through the cities and villages, journeying towards Jerusalem . . . . 'I must walk today and tomorrow and the day following, for it cannot be that a prophet perish out of Jerusalem!' . . . And there went a great multitude with him, and he turned [still striding ahead] and said to them, 'Whosoever does not bear his cross and come after me cannot be my disciple' . . . . It came to pass as he went to Jerusalem . . . . 'Behold, we go up to Jerusalem, and all things that are written shall be accomplished' . . . . He came nigh . . . entered and passed through Jericho . . . he was nigh unto Jerusalem and they thought the kingdom of God should immediately appear . . . . He went before, ascending up to Jerusalem . . .".

All such phrases, appearing thus consecutively in Luke's story, add to the sense of increasing pace, a "deliberate speed, majestic instancy", as Jesus advances upon the capital. Time is running out. Then, at the last provincial city, tension suddenly increases. A blind beggar by the wayside cries after Jesus for mercy and is healed, but the manner of the healing sends a thrill of excitement through disciples and bystanders: for Bartimaeus hailed Jesus as "Son of David" — and was not silenced. For the very first time Jesus had publicly accepted a messianic title without rebuke. The gauntlet was thrown, the issue joined. In every sense He had crossed His Jordan, and the final hour had struck.

II

Such is the prologue to the last great week of Jesus' life, and in its light His actions must be understood. We witness with increasing awe His fivefold challenge to Jerusalem to decide about Himself. Five deliberate, public, daring acts follow one upon another, like strokes on some reverberating gong announcing doom, until at last the rulers' hands are forced and, acting in haste and fear, they make their dreadful blunder.

(1) Within sight of the city and with deliberate timing, Jesus worked His greatest miracle of all, by raising Lazarus from the tomb. Not a Jew in Judea could fail to hear of it, and many flocked to Bethany to see Lazarus and speculate about Jesus. This stupendous deed, implying a no less astounding claim, defined the issues as surely as it set the stage for the offensive thus begun. The Lord of life and death offers to the nation life, or death, as they themselves shall choose.

(2) The debating crowds down from Jerusalem joined with the pilgrims coming up from Galilee for the Passover festival. Feast, crowds, miracle, and rumour conspire to kindle an excited fervour, both political and pious, and with consummate skill Jesus uses the occasion. Preparations were already made, a password had been arranged, and Jesus rode upon a borrowed colt up the royal and sacred way to the city gate.

All was as Zechariah the prophet had foretold: "Behold thy King cometh unto thee, meek and having salvation, lowly and riding upon an ass". Jesus was surrounded by the homage long ago offered to a king coming to his coronation, the strewing of garments in His way, the avenue of palms, the cries of the people. "Hosanna, welcome to the Son of David!" The whole episode was, and was seen to be, a direct and cleverly disguised claim to Kingship.

Yet Jesus came unarmed, in peace, escorted by pilgrims, riding on a humble donkey, and Rome is helpless. To treat this cavalcade as a serious menace to her power would be to invite ridicule! Yet Pharisees and scribes knew what He meant. Calling a council of action, they bitterly complained, "The whole world is gone after Him!"

(3) A fig tree stood by the wayside, familiar to thousands of the annual pilgrims. This year, as sometimes happened, the fruit "rested", though the leaves that normally followed the fruit appeared as usual. Suddenly the tree is withered, dying in a night. A city long familiar with prophetic symbolism, that expressed truth dramatically in deeds, needed no interpreter.

Leaves without fruit, ostentation without reality, profession without performance: a gorgeous Temple but no true worship, innumerable Passover pilgrims but little vital religion — and the end is death. A barren religion, a barren nation dies of its barrenness under the Word of God. So had Amos and Micah, Ezekiel and Isaiah shaken men's consciences with words of doom and deeds of vivid meaning; and Christ's act was understood.

(4) Pressing closer still to the heart of the nation, Jesus entered within the Temple precincts, and in one audacious act of righteous anger challenged the authority of the priestly families, publicly branding as thieves those who

waxed wealthy on the piety of the poor. Abuses were long standing. Only the priests could pass an animal for sacrifice, and it was therefore safer to buy in the first place from the priestly vendors; only Hebrew money was acceptable within the Temple, and priests fixed the rate of exchange for Roman coin.

For this profitable monopoly the priestly families took possession of the one place in Jerusalem where a Gentile or a stranger was permitted to say his prayers! No wonder Jesus took a whip to the beasts, overthrew the tables of the money-changers, and cried with all the passion of an ancient prophet, "It is written, My house shall be a house of prayer for all nations, but ye have made it a den of thieves!"

In face of such a mockery of worship, the spirit of Jesus blazed with such fierceness of denunciation that no one dared gainsay Him. But here was a challenge the authorities could not ignore, and when they had collected their wits and their courage, they charged Him with blasphemy against the Holy Place.

(5) Seated in the open courtyard of the Temple, surrounded by friends, antagonists, pilgrims, and sightseers, Jesus read aloud the solemn lesson of that exciting week. Choosing deliberately a much prized passage of Isaiah, which described the divine preparation, endowment, and care of the vineyard of Israel, Jesus so retold the story as to show how very little God had ever received from the appointed husbandmen. Prophet after prophet, and last of all God's well-beloved Son, had been sent to collect the harvest due. One after another had been ill-treated, threatened or slain. If indeed the Son is killed, then will God wrest the vineyard from the husbandmen of Israel, let it out to Gentiles, and take divine revenge.

The old theme of the beloved nation and the chosen plot is turned against Israel with a vengeance! This is blasphemy indeed, against Scripture, against the divine election, and against the hierarchy. Here, again, is the assumption of unique Sonship. "And the chief priests and the scribes the same hour sought to lay hands on him . . . for they perceived that he had spoken this parable against themselves."

By these five spectacular moves the master roused the city to fever-pitch and challenged the authorities to act;

in five successive hammer-blows upon the nation's conscience He sounded the fateful summons to — decide!

III

This picture of a Christ on the offensive is unfamiliar to us. Such relentless demand for decision accords ill with modern taste. We prefer blurred lines, wide tolerance; we hedge our opinions, insure our promises, analyse away as mere opinion-trends the great convictions that have driven men to noble deeds. We see all sides of every question except the answer. We cultivate a judgement in suspense, until the difference between right and wrong, truth and falsehood, disappears in a fog of figures about how many people any longer think that way!

In such a world of twilight and mist, where all roads are assumed to lead equally safely home — including the road to hell — Christ stands an uncompromising signpost, demanding a decision. He shatters our hesitations and complacency with His sharp insistence on a Yes or No, for God or against Him, for truth or error, for right or wrong, for Himself — or Satan.

God grant that unlike Jerusalem we each may know the day of our visitation, and the things that belong to our peace.

SUFFERING THAT ACHIEVES REDEMPTION

Final preparations
The Christian's Gethsemane
Who killed Jesus?
"Suffered under Pontius Pilate"
It is accomplished

21 Final Preparations

"With desire I have desired to eat this passover with you before I suffer."   Luke 22:15

THE QUIET CONVERSATION and moving scenes enacted in the upper room on the night that Jesus was betrayed represent perfectly the calm centre popularly supposed to lie at the heart of every storm.

The venue had been carefully arranged at some previous visit to the city. Two disciples are separated from the twelve and sent ahead to meet a stranger made conspicuous by carrying a water-pot. He leads them to the upper room, to prepare the Passover. Not until they arrive with Jesus do the rest know where the rendezvous is planned. All is reminiscent of "underground activity", but such care was necessary if Jesus were to spend even one night within the city undisturbed. There was a price upon His head.

When all is set, and Christ is ready, Judas is deliberately excluded. "What thou doest, do quickly" — and the traitor hurries off to reveal to the authorities where Jesus may be found.

Yet even as without in the sleeping city the plotting of the enemy proceeds and the tragedy hastens towards its end, within a scene of quiet beauty provides exquisite relief, and a perfect opportunity for the preparation of the eleven.

Nevertheless, Christ's theme is not approaching death, defeat, and darkness, but the challenging future and the tasks awaiting consecrated hearts.

The chapters that describe this intimate interlude are among the richest in all Scripture, but the main ideas are easily discerned. Jesus washes the disciples' feet, and calls for abiding loyalty through all the exacting years to come; He institutes the Supper, and He promises the Spirit.

I

Few acts, even of Jesus, excel in moral beauty His quiet acceptance of the servant's task at the Passover table, as He takes a towel and basin and performs the necessary cleansing. Probably none among the eleven would consent to have the purifying omitted; but none would lower himself to perform the menial service for the rest. Christ's action silently rebuked the strife among them about precedence. But it did more, as each man clearly understood.

Peter's protest against being washed by Jesus finds an echo in most hearts. For us to wash His feet, as Mary did, appears but right and fitting: if we do not imitate, we at least admire. But something in our pride and self-sufficiency rebels against admitting our need that He wash us. Give us a task to attempt, a cause to serve, and we will show what we can do. But we prefer not to be "beholden" — even to the mercy of God in Christ! Yet Jesus explicitly declares He came not to be served, but to serve, and firmly answers Peter in words with which we have to come to terms, "Except I wash thee, thou hast no part with me".

"I have given you an example, that ye should do as I have done to you." We like this even less; we are far readier to tread upon our fellows' toes, or step into their shoes, than we are to wash their feet. Such a command implies a willingness to serve without limit, without condescension, without self-flattering pride, without reward. It implies "in honour preferring one another" — Peter subservient to John, Matthew to James, and each of us to his rival, perhaps even his enemy.

We are all afraid we cannot afford this kind of thing. We get cynical and bitter about the sort of folk we deal with, jealous about our own prestige. He washed the feet of Peter, who denied; of Thomas who would doubt Him; of Judas who betrayed.

And so doing He set the example that embodies the whole ethic of the gospel — doing to others as He has done to us, giving as freely as we have received, serving as graciously as we have been served, loving as fully, as readily, as unquestioningly as He has first loved us. First to be cleansed, and then to serve the footsteps of our fellows — that is the simplest summary of the law of Christ.

II

The words about abiding in the vine take up again Isaiah's parable of the vineyard. The *new* Vine, planted and tended by the Father-Husbandman is not the nation, but Christ and His own. "I am the true vine, ye are the branches." But branches must adhere to the main trunk of the plant, else life cannot flow or fruit be borne. Judas already has severed his heart from Christ; hence he must wither and be pruned away. So will it be with all who fail to abide in the Vine.

This poetic idea is by no means vague, or mystic, or emotional. We abide in Christ, as His words abide in us, our minds attentive to His truth; as we continue in His love, not severed by unbelief; as His joy remains in us, guarded by obedience; as He Himself abides in prayerful hearts ever open to His fellowship.

Properly understood, this whole conception is startling, revolutionary. The entire purpose of God is now seen to rest upon a people united in mind and heart to Jesus. Religion consists henceforth no longer in national election or ritual tradition, or in legal faithfulness, but in unity with Christ. This "coming unto Him" in faith, and centring life upon Him, is salvation. Creed, ethic, ritual, and profession are all here made subordinate to relationship, to abiding in the Christ. The gospel's good news is just the offer of Christ to us to be this source and centre of our living. The gospel invitation is to come to Him, lay hold of Him, believe in Him, and so abide in Him.

For without Him we can indeed do nothing.

III

The exhortation to "abide in Christ" summarises perfectly the heart of three years' teaching; and the sacred meal that Jesus instituted in the upper room perpetuates just as perfectly the relationship that saves. Around that shared symbolic feast of broken bread and outpoured wine so many strands of Christian devotion, faith, and love have now been woven that it is easy to forget its immediate, urgent purpose.

The controlling circumstance is Jesus' imminent departure. It seems impossible that the disciples could ever forget Him, but they might; and others will arise with no personal memories of His earthly presence. Most sadly probably of all, men might misremember Him, each fashioning His memory in their own private image.

"This do," He said, "in remembrance of me." "This" is

the breaking of bread, the pouring of wine; and such actions fittingly symbolised the *character* in which He would be first remembered — as suffering Redeemer. Their individual participation in the elements sets forth the *way* in which He would be remembered, not in thought only but in full apprehension by the heart and spirit. His words about the covenant-blood assure them of His loyalty through the coming years; and the reminder that His blood is shed for the remission of sins keeps the whole relationship on its true foundation. The final words, about drinking with them in the Father's Kingdom, look beyond the travail and the waiting tasks to the End, when God shall reign and they shall sup again with Him in glory.

At the same time, by ancient and sacred codes of conduct in the East, the common meal is itself a solemn pledge of friendship and good faith between all who partake together. It is impossible to conceive any more powerful or effective means that Christ could have devised to perpetuate the relation of disciples to Himself, than this recurring feast of gratitude, memory, praise, and hope by which under many names and forms the whole Church remembers Him.

IV

But even the richest outward ceremony may become a meaningless rite, unless its true intention be scrupulously preserved. So Jesus added to the memorial Supper the glorious promise of the abiding Spirit.

This gift to them of His own Spirit would suffice for whatsoever the future brought, of persecution or of opportunity. Christ promises that He will not leave them "orphans". He will come to them, no longer in flesh and blood but in the Spirit, His "other Self". In all perplexities He will teach them, as the living Spirit of truth within each generation. In all their weakness He will equip them, as the living Spirit of power in every age. In all temptations He will keep them, as the Spirit of holiness within the Church. Through all changes and adjustments, in all dangers and achievements, He would be with them till the end of time.

He would abide in them even as they strove to abide in Him. They had His word that it would be so. And so have we.

Around these major themes is woven much of encouragement and warning, of comfort and appeal, of promise and assurance, as the Lord, intent upon His sacrifice, takes farewell of those He loves. A last memorable example which embodies all He taught of loving service to our fellows, a final moving exhortation that summarises perfectly His whole message, the sacred Supper that perpetuates relationship with Him, and the promise of His Spirit to endow for all the future days — such is the ample preparation through which He led His perplexed and wondering disciples in the quiet beauty of the upper room.

And without, through the darkened streets of the city, sped Judas to hasten on His death.

22 The Christian's Gethsemane

"I have trodden the winepress alone."   Isaiah 63:3

BEFORE HOFMANN'S magnificent painting of Christ in Gethsemane it is customary to kneel in silence. No other tribute seems adequate. In classic representations of the scene attention is drawn to the sleeping disciples: Hofmann makes them appear dimly in the background. Christ Himself rivets one's gaze, His uplifted face catching a beam from heaven — the one point of light amid deep gloom beneath the olive trees.

Thorns, rock, and storm-clouds recall with restrained symbolism the content of His prayer. On the distant horizon, wrapped in darkness, the outline of Jerusalem grimly reminds of what is in store. The disciples sleep. In God alone Christ's heart finds comfort and assurance.

In God alone: Gethsemane means "oil-press", and Christ's wistful request to the privileged three, "Tarry ye here and watch with me", recalls the prophet's cry: "I have trodden the winepress alone, and of the people there was none with me". For, like the prophet, Jesus enters upon His passion in intense loneliness of soul. Few details of the gospel narratives show His humanity, or suffering, with more aching poignancy than the request for human company in this waiting for the end. Few things can have caused the three more anguish of mind afterwards, than His sad rebuke, "What, could ye not watch with me one hour?"

Yet the wish for their companionship is not the whole meaning of His request. The re-interpretation of discipleship which began at Caesarea Philippi here reaches its most intense expression. On the way to the city Jesus had repeatedly warned of the perils involved; He had spoken of a baptism He must undergo, a cup of suffering He must drink, and of the disciples' share therein. In the upper room He had led them into closer identification with His passion in the broken bread and outpoured wine, though they were scarcely aware of all its implications. Now, in the moment of supreme spiritual anguish, when indeed the Sacrifice is laid upon the altar and bound there with the strong cords of His dedication and obedience, He would have the three who are nearest to His heart actually share the moment with Him.

They fail, through weakness and weariness of the flesh, and He endures the crisis utterly alone. Yet in some measure already they enter into His passion; they know it is their own pain that He bears, their own work He does, their own death He is about to die. In their name and on their behalf He offers Himself to God in sacrifice: inevitably they, and we, are in it with Him.

That is why, with profound theological and spiritual insight, the Church through many centuries has kept her own Gethsemane in the forty days of Lent, seeking by every sympathetic and symbolic means to watch with Christ in the darkness of the passion.

I

It is curious that Protestant churches have largely retained the great Christian festivals and rejected the great Christian fasts. Christmas and Easter are unceasingly celebrated, and with enormous zest and enthusiasm. Lent, Ash Wednesday, and Good Friday we are puzzled how to keep, or if we should.

Admittedly, it is very difficult to estimate the true religious value of the more rigorous calendar of spiritual training observed in the medieval Church. But there can be no doubt that much of the truth that sought expression in these older disciplines is urgently relevant to our modern situation. Our spiritual life would be immeasurably deeper, our Christian joy far more radiant, if something of the self-training in holiness, the austerity of dedication, the intentness of purpose in battling with world, flesh, and devil, which marked the medieval Church, lingered in our own.

We are an easygoing generation of Christians, on the whole, accomplished in the arts of compromise, broad in outlook, tolerant in morals, friendly even to the devil, and eager to present a warm, encouraging gospel with no edge of challenge, and no disturbing call to penitence or renunciation. We want a Christianity made easy for the multitude. Our just punishment, perhaps, is that we are left with precisely that.

To such minds the intellectual depth and moral demands of ancient liturgies and disciplines are repugnant, almost incomprehensible. But with Gethsemane and Calvary before us we know that we dare not be satisfied with this shallow Christian hedonism. We are compelled to ask ourselves whether we ought not to keep a Lenten fast of preparation in our very modern souls lest Jesus, finding us, too, asleep, should say, "Could ye not watch with me? The spirit truly is willing, but the flesh is weak; watch and pray that ye enter not into temptation".

II

Watch! — that call to Christian vigilance is one of the notes of permanent truth behind the Lenten custom. "What I say unto you I say unto all, Watch . . . . Watch therefore, for in such an hour as ye think not . . . . Watch ye, stand fast, be strong . . . . Let us watch and be sober . . . . Watch thou in all things."

It is instructive to notice how often the call to vigilance occurs in the New Testament. For it is very probable that the Apostolic Church possessed a pattern of instruction for her converts, roughly similar over most of the evangelised world, and that one whole section of it concerned this theme of the wide-awake mind, the unsleeping conscience, alert, on guard against insidious and infiltrating paganism.

Boyhood memories treasure an impression of an old magazine cover, showing a young knight kneeling before an altar, sword hilt upraised in steady hands, head bowed in prayer as he kept vigil against the powers of darkness for one long, lonely night, so earning the coveted title of Christian man-at-arms. The picture gathers into itself all the charm of the age of chivalry, the older ideal of the forty hours' vigil between Calvary and Easter which ancient Christians kept with the buried Christ, and the later forty days of watching, sorrow, and self-examination, which we call Lent.

We may smile at the romanticism. But the old call to Christian vigilance is a necessary protest against moral laxity, the easy neutralism which enervates much twentieth-century religion. Whether or not we want, we certainly need

> ... *a godly fear,*
> *A quick-discerning eye,*
> *That looks to Christ when sin is near*
> *And sees the tempter fly;*
> *A spirit still prepared,*
> *And armed with jealous care,*
> *For ever standing on its guard*
> *And watching unto prayer.*

III

The second note of permanent truth behind Lent's emula-
tion of Gethsemane is, of course, self-discipline. The old
antithesis still confronts us — willing spirit against weak
flesh, conscience against comfort, truth against expediency,
what we ought against what we like. Modern psychology
has confirmed a hundred times the Christian analysis of the
divided soul. Psychoanalysis has re-christened old insights
with new technical terms, but the ancient problems remain.

Man is two-sided. Man awakened to God has two natures:
the life of the spirit demands the surrender of the life of
the flesh. "I keep under my body, and bring it into sub-
jection . . . . So run that ye might obtain the prize . . . . Fight
the good fight, finish the course, endure hardness as a good
soldier of Jesus Christ." How can we have so far forgotten
the New Testament picture of the Christian athlete, stripped,
in training, laying aside every weight, hindrance, and dis-
traction, intent, concentrated, not beating the air, pressing
toward the mark for the prize of the upward calling, with
a crown to gain and a course to finish and a Master to
please?

Paul's great words about the Christian soldier, wrestler,
runner, boxer are exceedingly close in thought to the
Master's sayings about the strait gate and the narrow way;
about the denial of self that wins fuller life. And all such
ideals imply the prayer that makes salvation possible: "Not
my will, but thine, be done".

In an age confessedly hedonist in morals and thought, not
only the quality of Christianity but its very survival depends
on the positive, joy-affirming discipline of Christians in
defence of spiritual values, against the life-draining, empty,
embittering seductions of the flesh.

IV

But the strongest note of permanent truth behind Lent's participation in Gethsemane is our fellowship with Jesus in His passion. We speak, theologically, of Christ's death as "representative", as an expression in our name and on our behalf of a new attitude towards sin, an attitude that by His grace we will make our own. But this implies that ·we deliberately and with moral purpose identify ourselves with Him. We must say Amen to His atonement, stand in with Him in thus condemning and opposing sin. We must go on to know Him in the fellowship of His sufferings, "filling up that which is incomplete of the suffering of Christ", to borrow Paul's daring words. We are called to take upon ourselves some share of the travail that must be borne if the world is ever to be saved.

But this means tarrying with Him in Gethsemane. It means that by imaginative sympathy, by concrete sacrifices, by a living and personal concern, and by sustained and costly effort we enter practically into the redemptive passion of Jesus. Our little Lenten self-denials may be appallingly trivial, even hypocritical, or, by such vigilance, self-discipline, and fellowship in Christ's suffering, we may walk closely with Christ through Gethsemane to Golgotha.

> *Up to Mount Calvary*
> *If thou desir'st to go,*
> *Then take thy cross and follow Christ,*
> *Thou canst not miss it so!*

23 Who Killed Jesus?

"By wicked hands . . . . "   Acts 2:23

I

OF COURSE the soldiers did it. Doubtless, theirs was a limited responsibility; they were but tools in others' hands. Their duty bound them to obedience. Yet the refinements of cruelty which were added to the judicial sentence, the crown of thorns, the shabby robe, and the reed sceptre by which they made sport of His messianic claim, the buffeting and cruel game of "guess who hit you", and the final indignity of gambling beneath the cross to possess His clothes were their invention. If for the deed they can be excused, for the manner of it they cannot. They need not have enjoyed it.

Very occasionally we cannot help the things we have to do. A just verdict must be given, distasteful though the duty is. The criminal must be punished, the thriftless and dishonest refused public aid or indiscriminate charity, the enemy restrained by force, wrongdoing exposed, someone dismissed from employment. In such things often the real responsibility rests with others. Then more than ever must we watch the spirit in which we act. We may not shift unpleasant duties on to other shoulders, and if we cannot justly decline, we must see that the hard thing is done with the utmost care and kindness the case allows.

If our situation be still more compromising, and the things we have to do be wholly wrong, then Christian loyalty dictates that at whatever cost to career, ambition, and income, or in ridicule, we *get out*.

II

Long before Jesus passed into the soldiers' hands, the Jerusalem crowd had done their part. After three years of selfless ministry and incomparable teaching, Jesus was hounded to death by those He had served and loved. Nothing can excuse the people of Jerusalem for that cry of "crucify him" following so soon upon "Hosanna" and the "hearing him gladly" when in the Temple He discomforted the scribes.

Jesus had been too truthful a teacher, too spiritual a Messiah, too realistic and exacting a religious leader to please the mob. Barabbas was much more to the crowd's liking: a man of large promises of revolution, of violent action and bold challenge to Rome. With want of perception and base ingratitude must be ranked the strange mercurial emotion which makes everybody's deed seem no one's personal responsibility.

Yet the crowds were certainly responsible. Their earlier favour towards Jesus, when Galilean pilgrims helped to swell their number, had hitherto restrained the authorities from taking action, lest rioting break out. Only when, with the Galileans lodging beyond the city walls, Caiaphas could present an early-morning city-mob with a *fait accompli,* and represent Pilate's hesitation as a denial of Jewish rights, did the crowd turn against Jesus to get the better of the governor. Such was their influence, for protection and for destruction. Though every individual would disclaim his share in that morning's dark events, submerging his conscience in the general clamour, yet each in that crowd stands clearly condemned.

"Well, many do it" is no excuse, or shelter: it may well be sufficient reason for assuming it is wrong.

III

Neither soldiers nor crowd would have found opportunity had it not been for Judas. Historically, he has borne most of the blame for Jesus' death, but the stage was set for judicial murder and a price was placed on Jesus' head before Judas intervened. One difficulty remained, how Jesus might be arrested without uproar at Passover-time. This, Judas solved, betraying to the authorities the fact that Christ had stayed within the city after sundown, and where He might be found.

So before the crowd could interfere, Jesus was in custody, tried, condemned, and standing at daybreak in Pilate's hall, to become an issue between Jewish and Roman authority and prestige.

Three things sharpen the responsibility of Judas: the

opportunities Jesus gave him, the unfailing love that Jesus showed to him, and his own pretended loyalty. Just why he betrayed his Master is not easy to explain. Behind his action probably lie bitter, humiliating disappointment of golden ambitions and a burning patriotism that cherished thwarted ideas of a kingdom and a crown. The realisation that Jesus meant to reign "only" in men's hearts by love left a sense of grievance that hungered for reprisal. Covetousness — blood brother to ambition — and a thief's squalid spirit (John says) made him determined to gain at once his own security and the proffered bribe. For thirty pieces of silver Judas sold his Lord, his honour, and his life.

His part was minor, but his guilt was great. He stands for ever as history's darkest example of an essentially trivial yet treacherous betrayal.

IV

Far more dangerous, and culpable, was the duplicity of Caiaphas, High Priest of Jewry and ruthless, calculating leader of the ruling clique. Angered at Christ's criticisms, jealous of His influence, blind to His credentials, Caiaphas secretly arrested Jesus, stooping to bribery to do so. He tried Him, illegally, during hours of darkness, appointing himself both judge and prosecutor, calling witnesses and then choosing to ignore their contradictory testimony. He allowed no defence, made no investigation, and challenged Jesus, again illegally, to condemn Himself by unsupported confession.

Caiaphas sentenced Christ to death for blasphemy, but changed the charge to treason in order to gain Pilate's confirmation. Giving a meaning to Christ's words which Caiaphas well knew to be false, he blackmailed Pilate into acquiescence, and incited the people to desire that Barabbas — a *proved* traitor — should be released and Jesus crucified.

For ruthless cunning, falsehood, cynicism, and selfish diplomacy, Caiaphas stands condemned. Blind loyalty to traditional religion, good or bad, and concern for the safety of the Jewish state were his motives: and insincere religion plus cynical statecraft make a fearful combination for evil. In the eyes of Caiaphas, to get rid of Jesus would preserve the existing compromise with Rome, save the Jewish institutions, the ruling class, his own job, and end the whole dangerous messianic movement that had begun with John. That it involved judicial murder was unfortunate; that it meant silencing the greatest prophetic voice heard in Israel for centuries, Caiaphas did not notice!

Expediency can represent any wrong as right, miscall murder patriotism, and invent virtuous excuses for vicious things. As so often, it was in Caiaphas' case lamentably shortsighted. The nearer danger, that of Rome, hid from him the ultimate peril, the judgement of God. He played Rome's game for her, and in forty years Rome destroyed everything he was seeking to preserve. It is indeed a strange expediency that fears Caesar more than God.

V

The ultimate responsibility for Jesus' death rests on Pilate. As he said to Jesus, he alone had final authority to condemn. The charge read: "He calleth himself Christ, a king, forbidding to give tribute to Caesar"; but during cross-examination Jesus gave the satisfactory answer, "My kingdom is not of this world". His was the moral authority of truth, not the political authority of thrones and governments. And His bearing impressed Pilate as deeply as His words.

Pilate knew well that Christ was innocent. Three times he declared, "I find no fault in Him". Yet fearing to anger the Jews, he hedged and hesitated. The High Priest's subtle warning, "If thou let this man go, thou art not Caesar's friend", implied the awful threat of yet another Jewish complaint to Caesar, and an imperial enquiry into his governorship. This he could not face. Only three years later such an investigation into his record led to his removal in disgrace.

Thus Pilate's hand was forced, by the clamour of the crowd, the cleverness of Caiaphas, and the consequences of his own past rule. Repeatedly he sought to evade decision, sending Jesus to Herod as a Galilean, offering to release Him as the Passover amnesty, compromising by unjustly scourging Jesus, then washing his hands of the whole affair. But nothing availed. Cornered and blackmailed, to save his own position Pilate yielded Jesus to their will; how sullenly, the inscription above the cross, "King of the Jews", and the bad-tempered refusal to alter it, plainly show.

It is easy to find excuses for Pilate, but he stands condemned by his own affirmations of Christ's innocence, by his vacillations and evasions, by his cowardly sacrifice of Christ to his own interests. Appointed, trained, and trusted to administer justice, he failed at what should have been his strongest point. For moral cowardice deliberately sacrificing the innocent for selfish ends, Pilate stands eternally responsible for Jesus' death.

VI

So Jesus died. A little cruel sport, some thoughtless ingratitude and mob emotion, frustrated ambition linked to avarice, blind, cynical expediency, moral cowardice saving its own skin and the Christ of God is crucified. Small infidelities betray great causes; the little sins of many breed colossal corporate tragedy.

Nevertheless, when all is said, though men acted in the freedom and responsibility of their own volition, yet Jesus was not their passive Victim. Foreseeing, knowing, accepting all, He followed with unfaltering step the path of loyalty to duty, truth, and God, and laid down His life. To the deed of the soldiers, the demand of the people, the disappointment of Judas, the duplicity of Caiaphas, the decision of Pilate must be added, to make the story quite complete, the dedication of Jesus to the redemption of mankind. When all the historic causes are analysed and tabulated, and their solemn lessons learned, it still is true

> *He died that we might be forgiven,*
> *He died to make us good:*
> *That we might go at last to heaven,*
> *Saved by His precious blood.*

24 "Suffered under Pontius Pilate"

"They saw that he was dead already."
"When Jesus had cried with a loud voice, he said, Father, into thy hands I commend my spirit: and having said this, he gave up the ghost."
"Not by water only, but by water and blood."

John 19:33, Luke 23:46, I John 5:6

For FIFTEEN HUNDRED years the Church has declared its faith in a pattern of statements known as the "Apostles' Creed". It contains some twenty-one affirmations, beginning with "I believe in God the Father Almighty . . ." and ending with "the life everlasting"; and of these twenty-one no less than thirteen concern Jesus; five — a quarter of the whole Christian creed — centre around His suffering. Jesus "suffered under Pontius Pilate, was crucified, dead, and buried; He descended into hell".

So firmly and repeatedly is the cross of Jesus written into the heart of Christian faith, as its symbol is woven into the fabric of its shrines, and its memory into the pattern of Christian worship.

I

At first sight it might appear that the Church is labouring the obvious. But it must be remembered that the creed was framed defensively, to guard the faith against misunderstanding and deliberate heresy. The five affirmations about the cross are fences erected to preserve the essential truth against distortion and denial.

Some early Christians, for example, found it hard to believe that God's Son could actually suffer. The First Epistle of John and certain verses in John's Gospel, refer to this stumbling block to faith. To avoid an idea so untenable as a suffering divinity, these thoughtful folk suggested that Christ only *seemed* to suffer, or that someone else, perhaps Simon of Cyrene, suffered for Him, or the divine Christ left the human Jesus in the Garden of Gethsemane, and only the "human" Jesus died.

Against all this "Christian science" the Church set resolutely the plain and startling fact that Jesus Christ, the Son of God, *suffered*. She dated it, "under Pontius Pilate"; she located it, in Judea where Pilate governed; she explained it, as enforced by Rome; she reiterated it in fivefold repetition to make quite clear that *Jesus suffered*.

With equal realism the Church refused to dilute the awful truth by "spiritualising" Christ's agony. It is perfectly true that the passion included more than physical pain. The sacrifice involved in Christ's becoming man at all, the rejection and ingratitude of those He served, the constant strife and controversy, the vicarious suffering of a felt sympathy with men and ceaseless labour on their behalf, loneliness, ill-will, injustice, betrayal — all added to His suffering. But He was *crucified*: the creed repeats it endlessly, lest in the abstractions of theory and the sentiment of poetry the stark fact of His agony be disguised.

If modern taste has turned from the awful portrayals of that agony in earlier Christian art, still "the most cruel and most horrible of tortures" retains its place in Christian thought. We dare not sentimentalise the pain of Jesus, lest an inhuman callousness make us insensitive to the pain of other hearts.

It seems hardly necessary to add that He *was dead;* but the problem here was to make palatable the idea of bodily resurrection. Those who delight to make faith easy, and clear the way for facile "explanations" of hard things, were busy enough with theories: Christ was taken from the cross too soon; He fainted, and was laid within the tomb unconscious but not dead. His strength returning, He broke the seals from within! With the gospel narratives, the eye-witnesses' account, the mourning disciples, and the governor's edict all behind her, the Church replies that He *was dead*.

To leave no shred of doubt she adds, *and buried*. Here was no mystic translation, like that of Enoch, no ascension to heaven in a chariot of fire as with Elijah, no stealing of His body by disciples. The seals, the guards, the spices of the women, and the startled incredulity of the disciples three days later tell another tale. They emphasise beyond question that Christ "was dead, and buried".

The final underlining of the harsh fact is strangest of all: He *descended into [hades] hell,* abode of the dead awaiting final judgement. "Thou wilt not leave my soul in hades" said the Psalmist, and Peter applied the words to Jesus. "Who shall descend into the abyss, that is to bring Christ up from the dead?" asks Paul; "that he ascended, what is it but that he also descended first into the lower parts of the earth?" "He came and preached to the spirits in prison" says Peter obscurely.

We are here in a realm defying definition and imagination. We must be content with the hints and implications of the Biblical writers and, refusing speculation, attend rather to the purpose behind this emphasis on the fulness of Christ's experience of death. No foothold for doubt, no loophole for evasion, is permitted. The actual, literal, horrible death of Jesus is insisted upon as essential to the Church's faith and message.

"Jesus suffered under Pontius Pilate, was crucified, dead, and buried; He descended into hell." That such a fact should need such reiteration is itself important evidence of how men thought of Jesus. To them it was astonishing, and almost unbelievable, that such as He should die.

II

There is, however, much more at stake in the defensive phrasing of the creed than just replying to doubts about the details of the story. In these five affirmations the meaning of Christ's Saviourhood and the significance of His suffering are likewise being declared.

He suffered. Therein lies comfort, enlightenment, and hope for all who are afflicted. Suffering henceforth holds no baffling contradiction of the Father's love, points no accusing finger, is no proof of sin. "He suffered, though a Son, learning obedience by the things which he suffered." Yet in His suffering He trusted, and hoped, and was sustained. In His faith and patience generations of the godly have found, if not an answer to their questions, a superb inspiration for their hearts in days and nights of pain.

He was crucified. Therein lies endurance for all who are persecuted, for all who in doing good are rejected and opposed, dishonoured and ill-treated. Jewish persecutors accomplished His death and pagans designed the manner of it; and from that time the cross has been the badge of truth unflinchingly defended whatever the consequences, of right unswervingly upheld whatever the opposition, of service and love undiscourageably pursued whatever the ingratitude or cost. "Marvel not if the world hate you," Jesus said, "it hated me . . .".

He died. Therein lies hope for all who fear the valley of the shadow. He is the Christ of the darkest hour and the final dread, destroying by His own death him that hath the power of death, and liberating those "who through fear of death were all their lifetime subject to bondage". His promises are backed by His experience and triumph: "This day thou shalt be with me in paradise . . . . I will come again and receive you unto myself". As Maclean Watt finely pleads,

> *Carry me over the long, last mile,*
> *Man of Nazareth, Christ for me!*
> *Weary I wait by death's dark stile*
> *In the wild and the waste where the wind blows free. . . .*
>
> *Lord, is it long that my spirit must wait?*
> *Man of Nazareth, Christ for me!*
> *Deep is the stream, and the night is late,*
> *And grief blinds my soul, for I cannot see.*
>
> *Speak to me out of the silences, Lord,*
> *That my spirit may know*
> *As forward I go,*
> *That Thy pierced hands are lifting me over the ford.*

It is no longer the rod and staff alone that give us courage, but the Christ Himself, going with us through the darkness and there to greet us on the other side. For Jesus "was dead"

He was buried. And with Him was buried all the hope and happiness of those who loved Him. Mary lingered broken-hearted at the tomb; Peter remained alone, uncomforted; John's heart was desolate. Two walked to Emmaus perplexed and savouring despair. All faced alike the awful finality of the tomb — only to discover that "gates of brass before Him burst, iron fetters yield", and

> *Death is but a covered way*
> *To life, and everlasting day.*

For all who stand in grief beside a grave and see an empty future stretch before, there is balm, steadiness, and light in the sombre words, "He was buried".

He descended into hell. The after-life is somehow less mysterious, less lonely and forbidding, since He went on ahead. This is the spiritual purpose which the obscure doctrine serves. He is the Christ of time — of all the times, and of eternity — the Christ within the Father's house, Christ with us to the end that has no end. To Him, says Paul, every knee shall bow . . . of things under the earth; to this end Jesus died and rose again, that He might be Lord both of the dead and of the living — for all live unto Him. Through time and through eternity His cross still judges and still saves: therein is assurance and victory for all who face the unknown in His name.

III

Thus carefully does the Church define and jealously defend her faith in Calvary. This emphasis on the passion is certainly less central in modern Christianity than once it was. Such concentration on the darker side of life is distasteful to modern feeling, incomprehensible to modern minds, repulsive to modern pride. For we moderns choose to live in dream-worlds of fiction, glamour, wealth, ease, romance, and happy endings.

The Church has ever been more realistic and more truthful. Suffering, sin, fear, mortality, and despair lurk not far below the surface even of modern hearts; and for such needs there is a message of a Saviour who has gone the whole way through in identifying Himself with man. From the centre of His agony, from the very darkness of His tomb, He offers life and peace and hope.

> *A Christless cross no refuge were for me:*
> *A crossless Christ — no Saviour would He be:*
> *But, O Christ crucified, I rest in Thee!*

25 It Is Accomplished

"My Father worketh."
"My meat is . . . to finish his work."
"It is finished."

John 5:17, 4:34, 19:30

ONE OF THE MOST daring products of the ever lively Greek imagination is the story of the labours of the hero Hercules. The fable ventures to set a god to work; it presumes to describe tasks worthy the attention of a son of Zeus. He strangles snakes within his cradle, slays with bare hands the Nemean lion, kills the nine-headed serpent, captures the fleet-footed, golden-horned stag, obtains the golden apples of the Hesperides, cleanses the foul Augean stables by the diversion of a river. All is done with incredible strength and courage, and a great deal of magic.

Beneath the flights of fancy is some serious thought. The labours of Hercules involve the removal of monsters that prey upon human life, the capturing of lovely but unattainable things, the cleansing away of foulness, the invasion of hades to challenge the power of death. Equally significant, all is done in penance, to atone for the frenzied killing of his own children.

One senses behind the tales the sad experience of humanity — of things mercilessly destructive, things desirable but out of reach, things that defile, the fear of death, and the need of atonement. One senses, too, an elementary faith that divine strength may accomplish what man unaided cannot do.

So Greeks dreamed. But the dangers, problems, frustrations, and fears that beset mankind are similar in all lands and times. Hebrews, too, conceived God as labouring "with a mighty hand and an outstretched arm", at the colossal task imposed on the divine wisdom by man's predicament. This is the work which Jesus said "the Father hath given me to finish". Here is truly Herculean toil: to cleanse the foul stables of the world with the river of God's grace, destroy the menace that imperils man's true welfare, break open the gates of death, and recapture the golden apple of eternal life.

The whole Bible is the record of that agelong toil of

love. "My Father worketh," Jesus declares, "and I work; my meat is . . . to finish his work; I must work the works of him that sent me." Later Jesus prays concerning "the work which thou gavest me to do": in death He cries triumphantly, "It is accomplished".

All that God could do to save mankind was done, when Jesus died. What was accomplished? What tasks could Hebrew minds conceive as worthy of a God?

I

Looking back through Scripture from the vantage point of Calvary, where the work was finished, it is clear that one strange work that needed to be done, to save the world from its predicament, was to make plain to man that God hates sin.

Odd though it seems now, it was entirely characteristic of pagan thought to impute evil to the universe itself, ascribing every wickedness to the gods. To combat relentlessly that ultimate blasphemy was one of the glories of the Old Testament. Law, precepts, ritual, sacrifice, prophecies and warnings, the long discipline of history and the sharp lessons of experience — all were consciously directed to teach that *God is holy*. The divine resistance to sin is one of the major themes of Scripture: the everlasting opposition of right and wrong, truth and falsehood, good and evil, man's wilfulness and God's will.

Sometimes that cosmic conflict is represented as a mere trial of strength. But the deepest Scriptural insight soon perceives that God's hostility to sin must, if man is ever to be saved, be worked out within humanity, on moral terms. And that meant incarnation, a sinless life, and an atoning death.

So in Jesus the divine resistance to evil reached its zenith. The massive strength of Christ was dedicated to the assertion of God's truth in face of all earth's lies, the enforcement of God's rule in face of man's rebellion. Within His own character, He resisted sin's allurement by staunch rejection of all temptation. Within the lives of others He resisted evil's power and fascination by His own endless patience, forgiving grace, and loving friendship. Within society at large He resisted its intimidation and violence

by consenting unto death. He died unembittered, unde-
feated, refusing to yield.

All this was mirrored in the inevitable collision between
Christ and all that Caiaphas, Pilate, Judas, Jewry, and Rome
defended. Had Jesus trimmed His words, abated His claims,
softened His criticisms, evaded the outright challenge, the
tragic outcome *might* have been avoided. But evasion, neu-
trality, and compromise involved base treachery to His
Father. The final week of open war but focusses His whole
life's unrelenting opposition to whatever would dispute
His Father's Kingship. Evil must be exposed as rebellion
against Love — that is Christ's first work.

Until man sees evil in its true light, he cannot be saved
from its enticements. By resolutely confronting evil with
an implacable will, Jesus expressed the divine reaction
against sin. By setting in contrast to it His own goodness,
patience, grace, and love, He revealed its true malignancy.
By refusing to descend to its own level and fight with its
own weapons He made plain for all time its essential
wrongness, its ultimate futility. Never again can man doubt
the nature of evil or God's hostility to it. That work is
finished, on the cross. Evil stands eternally condemned
by what it did to Jesus.

II

Yet man is not saved by revulsion alone: he must see
God. Here is a real problem of communication, of getting
past man's mistrust and fear and rebellious resentment to
make him understand, and then believe. This, too, in
Scriptural eyes, was a Godlike labour.

The Old Testament writers use every artifice of poetry,
ridicule, argument, law, ritual, and promise to free the
idea of God from its degradation in the sensual idolatry of
surrounding peoples. Through law and prophets and liturgy
there emerges the truth that God is one, holy, wise, infinite,
majestic, and worthy of man's worship. He is Lord, of
nature, history, and the whole earth; He is Lord, too, of
conscience; He is the Creator, King and Judge of men.

In passages of infinite tenderness God is also the fount
of everlasting mercy, whose inmost nature is "steadfast loving-
kindness", and whose unchanging will is every man's salvation.

But the task of revelation was focussed and finalised again in a human life, in Jesus. Before Christ all earlier revelation pales. He is "the outshining of the Father's glory, the express image of his person". Jesus can say: "No man knoweth the Father save the Son, and he to whomsoever the Son will reveal him". He even adds: "He that hath seen me, hath seen the Father". This was a supreme task set for Jesus: to make God really known, banishing man's foolish unbelief, imagined resentment, wilful rebellion, reconciling men to God in trust, in love, in peace, and joyful rest.

Christ's own presence among men is in itself the final revelation. He is God's compassion movingly expressed. But the revelation is written large in suffering, shame, rejection, and sin. It is nowhere more clear than at the end:

> Inscribed upon the cross we see
> In shining letters, "God is love".

That is the magnet by which He draws all men to come and see what God is like. That is the window He provides into eternity. That is the last satisfying word from God to men. God Himself can say no more, but

> Show you sweet Jesu's wounds, poor, poor dumb mouths
> And bid them speak,

putting a tongue in every wound that should move the stones of Rome to rise to a doxology.

For the second divine task, of making God known, reaches its consummation on the cross.

III

Looking back once more from the vantage point of Calvary, back through the long story of God's work in history, we realise that there is another task ascribed to God. From Noah and the ark, from Abraham and the covenant, from Moses and the exodus to law and sacrifice, psalms of the divine mercy, and promises of the deliverer, the idea that monopolises Scripture is the idea of man's redemption.

Old Testament and New Testament alike insist that salvation, redemption, deliverance, is God's work: it originates in the divine initiative of grace, to which man is called to respond by faith, acceptance, and obedience. The task is God's: and into it Christ has entered as at once God's

Representative and man's Saviour. He came to call sinners to repentance, to give His life a ransom for many, to shed His blood for the remission of sins, and as the good Shepherd to give His life for the sheep.

These are Christ's own definitions of His work. Something needed doing that man could not do, something that even Christ could not do by illuminating words and kindly deeds alone. Some satisfaction due to the imperative demands of eternal righteousness, some act of universal penitence, some deed of atonement and reconciliation was due from us and beyond our power to accomplish. This He made His work, serving our need, paying our debt, ransoming our souls, obtaining our remission, achieving redemption.

And that work He declares is done, completed, perfectly accomplished — as He dies. "It is finished."

IV

Thus the cross of Jesus is the real end of the Scripture story of God's labours in the resistance to evil, the revelation of love, and the redemption of man. All the rest is concerned with telling what God has done, and experiencing its power.

But this is the central, provocative paradox at the heart of the Christian evangel. We look about us at a world whose salvation seems scarcely to have begun, where all the big problems wait upon solution and all the great tasks wait attempting; a world in which men live as though God did not care, or did not matter, and the ancient evils still hold sway. And in this unsaved world we proclaim a *finished* work!

In spite of all appearances, that is the final truth. Never can evil be more ruthlessly exposed; never can God's love more perfectly be seen; nothing remains to be done to make possible man's return to God — except man's acceptance of the work.

That is the stumbling block. God can do no more: that is why the cross is judgement; refused, it is the end of hope. Christ need do no more; that is why the cross is blessed assurance; accepted, it is the end of all our painful, fearful effort to save ourselves. But the price to be paid is our pride in ourselves. It could not be otherwise. The essence of all sin is man's pride in himself, asserted in his boasted independence of divine aid, expressed also in his boasted freedom of self-will. It is therefore inconceivable that man could be saved from sin and leave his pride intact!

So God alone must save: man is left nothing to glory in, save the cross of the Lord Jesus Christ. The work is done— but not by us. Ours is but to accept, in humility, gratitude, and answering love.

Triumph that Transfigures Tragedy

Christ is risen!
"If Christ be not raised . . ."
Brave new world indeed
Ascension to pre-eminence
The great commission

26 *Christ Is Risen!*

THE FIRST CHRISTIANS believed that Jesus rose again because they met Him. Argue as we will about the self-vindicating documents, or the philosophical consequences of belief, the only final evidence of truth is personal encounter. "We have seen the Lord" is at once the beginning of faith and the end of all debate. If Christ be not available, accessible, apprehended now in our time in personal experience, it matters little whether the tomb was empty. What the heart sorely needs, and faith urgently demands, is not just a doctrine of the resurrection but a living Lord.

This is precisely what the first Easter brought to the earliest Christian believers. Each separate experience of those thrilling forty days centres in a face-to-face encounter with the risen Christ. Christ meets the women, who hastened from the tomb, with His glad "All hail"; He calls Mary by her name; He joins the sad conversation of the two walking to Emmaus. The perplexity of Peter and John in the garden is resolved when He comes to meet the eleven at evening, as the doubt of Thomas was answered not by reasons but by personal manifestation. The lakeside in Galilee, the upper room in Jerusalem, and the hillside above Bethany are places made forever memorable by the touch of His immortal feet, the thrill of His undying presence. In the last resort, then as now, the unanswerable evidence of the resurrection of the Crucified is the risen Christ.

I

Among these personal manifestations of the risen Lord are four private, individual, unexpected interviews that hold especial significance for us today, for between them they make clear the manner and conditions of such experience.

One is most briefly recounted: "He was seen of James". When, where, and by what means we are not told. The effect we know, the reason we must conjecture. Before Calvary none of Christ's family was found among the twelve. Most thought Him mad, and sought once to protect Him from Himself. So Mary His mother was committed at the end to the care of John and not to His brethren. But afterwards, James is prominent in the church, becoming famed for piety and prayerfulness.

Christ showed Himself to none in unbelief, refusing still to coerce faith by supernatural display. When Jesus appeared to him, James was evidently somewhere between unbelief and faith: the interview served to nourish and confirm a faith but just begun, and willing still to grow.

The second private interview is likewise barely mentioned. When two run rejoicing from Emmaus to Jerusalem, they find the disciples discussing an appearance of Jesus unto Peter. That is all we know. What Jesus said to the shame-faced disciple, what Peter stammered out at this first meeting since his own denial, we cannot guess. But Peter is found again with the eleven when evening comes, so far restored, forgiven, and renewed.

The third personal interview is unforgettably described. Mary, "out of whom" Mark remembers at a strangely inappropriate moment "Jesus cast seven devils", lingers in the garden, her desolate grief clinging passionately to the place where last she had seen her Lord. Through blinding tears she fails to recognise the Master, until He speaks. Then all is changed — breathing only the adoring "Rabboni", she worships Him.

About each of these stories there is a reticence befitting experiences too sacred to tell easily. The fourth is very different. Paul rides to Damascus bent on persecuting Christians, but experiencing already within himself the pricking of Christ's goad, the ferment of Christ's truth, the haunting grace of the dying Stephen at whose martyrdom he had himself assisted. Suddenly Christ appears. Paul's soul is "apprehended", his resistance crumbles, and from a smitten, surrendered heart Paul cries, "*Lord*, what wilt thou have me to do?"

So to James and Peter, to Mary and to Paul the truth of the resurrection is brought home by transforming encounter with the risen One. James' great need was to learn the truth, to find the divine wisdom that he later writes about, that could see his Brother as his Lord. An agony of doubt, we may suppose, was set aside by certainty.

Peter's great need was to find forgiveness, to be reinstated, comforted, and saved from self-reproach and crippling despair. His agony of penitence was set aside by pardon.

Mary's greatest need was consolation, to rediscover strength, calmness, and new hope. Her agony of sorrow, her heavy aching loneliness of heart, was set aside by finding Him alive forevermore.

Paul's great need was mastery. Within his soul — he later writes — the evil that he hated reigned in his emotions, the good he longed to follow was defeated by the flesh. In an agony of self-divisive conflict he needed most of all a Lord worthy to command and powerful to redeem.

Each found at once, for ever, in the risen living Christ the all-sufficient answer to his need. They knew He was alive by what He did for them.

II

But need is not enough, else would all have seen the Saviour. Why did He come especially to these? What in them beside their need made possible this glorious privilege and joy? The answer is illuminating.

James typifies the enquiring mind, the teachable, humble spirit. This we know from the letter he wrote long afterwards, revealing not only the quality of his thought but a mind steeped and saturated in the words of Jesus. Well over fifty echoes of the sayings of Christ have been counted in James' five short chapters — evidence sufficient of the earnest study and long reflection which James had given to the Master's message.

Peter was prepared for the encounter by self-accusing, broken-hearted penitence. His vision was cleansed by the "weeping bitterly" which followed his denial. None, in any age, have seen the living Christ more clearly than they who have sought Him through repentant tears: that is why those whose lives have been redeemed from the darkest sin are firmest in their conviction and ready to shout the loudest that "Jesus lives!"

Mary's preparation to see the Lord was just devoted love, anguished at Christ's absence, satisfied with His presence, seeking nothing but to have Him near, wanting Him not just for blessing's sake but for His own.

Paul's was a heart long ploughed with deep thought, high striving, dark defeat, and passionate sincerity. No one who listens to his testimony can doubt the painful road he travelled ere Christ appeared to him; no one who measures his accomplishment can question that out of deep conflict he attained his vigorous strength, his powerful faith, his all-enduring loyalty.

Such attitudes of mind and soul are crucially important if we are ever to know the truth about the Christ. There is a doubt that, unlike James', is unteachable and proud: to it the risen Lord is never known. There is a despair that, unlike Peter's, is hard and rebellious: to it the risen Lord can never come. There is a sorrow that, unlike Mary's, grows embittered, cynical, self-pitying, and to it Christ cannot convey His infinite comforting. There is fierce conflict that turns sceptical and careless, and it learns nothing of Christ's power.

But when within the doubt there abides a searching mind in love with truth, when beneath despair there lurks a penitent, longing spirit, when behind the sorrow there beats a loving heart, and through all the bitter conflict there remains an earnest will *wanting* to be obedient, there Christ can make His presence known, reveal His hands and side, and speak again His "Peace be unto you!"

III

There is, of course, much more that must be said about the Easter faith and Easter questionings. But essentially, religious truth is personal assessment, and the road to understanding lies not through argument but through discovery, made in action rather than in contemplation. Christian truth is *living* truth: it "comes alive" in life, and only rarely in discussion. The risen Christ still shows Himself, rarely to those who sit cleverly debating theoretic possibilities about survival, but often to those personally involved in searching after truth to live by, in wrestling heroically with despair, in preserving a passionate, devoted love for the best that they have known, in earnest moral conflict.

Hence it is that men and women surest of the risen Christ are those most deeply implicated in the Christian cause. Paul's thrice repeated testimony to the risen Master's presence well illustrates the essential truth. It was in prison in Jerusalem awaiting trial, on board a storm-tossed ship a prisoner conveyed to Rome, and then again in Caesar's court awaiting verdict, that Paul could say, "The Lord stood by me". It is men like St. Vincent, serving in the galleys among criminals and slaves, Luther confronting Europe with unwelcome truth, Damien whitening among his lepers, Judson languishing in a Burma jail, Rutherford imprisoned in Edinburgh, Bunyan in a Bedford cell, Livingstone dying in the bush, Paton burying his own wife in a lonely foreign grave, Kagawa plunging headlong into Tokio's slums, George Young toiling in perilous war-torn China, and hosts of other committed, active, dedicated souls, who are the living witnesses to the living Christ in every generation. They, who chose to become *involved,* have seen the Lord.

Academic discussion about the Easter probabilities may clear the ground of needless obstacles, but for personal conviction a personal commitment is essential. Life is very different from thinking about life; the arena and not the balcony is the place of discovery. Speculative debate about what might conceivably be true is of little value to hearts hungry for a faith to give life meaning. The cleverest minds may lose Him in the argument, where honest enquiry, simple penitence, deep devotion, sincere surrender will cry with passionate conviction and abounding joy: "Christ is risen: we have seen the Lord!"

27 "If Christ be not raised...."

"If Christ be not risen, then is our preaching vain, and your faith is also vain. . . . If Christ be not raised . . . ye are yet in your sins. Then they also which are fallen asleep . . . are perished . . . . we are of all men most miserable."

I Corinthians 15:14, 17, 18, 19

A DEEPLY MOVING beauty of expression and a striking reticence of description in the gospel narratives of the resurrection match their immeasurable importance; but no less impressive is their air of utter astonishment. A certain naive simplicity in the telling enables us still to feel the amazed bewilderment in which the eleven disciples spent the world's first Easter Day.

Facile explanations of the story which suppose it was invented in honour of Jesus (!) by over-credulous disciples are only plausible so long as one carefully avoids reading the only historical sources we possess. Everything in the record underlines the fact that, in spite of all the promises which they *afterwards* recalled, these men were taken entirely unprepared. So far from inventing the resurrection, they themselves had first to be persuaded of its truth, against their inclination and, in Thomas' case at least, against their will.

I

This initial astonishment was compounded of sadness, fear, and unbelief. Overwhelming grief marks the sorrowful procession that winds through the garden to the sepulchre at daybreak on the first day of the week. Infinite sadness makes Mary linger at the tomb, her eyes too filled with tears to recognise the Lord. Later, when she tells her story, it is to "them that had been with him, as they mourned and wept". Two others walk to Emmaus arguing, sad, dispirited, disappointed. Neither Peter nor Thomas are found at first within the company, and the odd phrase "found the disciples *gathered together*" suggests the disciple band had begun already to break up in disillusion and despair.

Fear, too, is everywhere. "Fear not" is the first word spoken

154

by the Easter angels, and fear is the first of all reactions to the Easter fact. "They departed from the sepulchre with fear" — the "great joy" came only later. "They trembled and were amazed . . . . They were terrified and affrighted . . . . They supposed that they had seen a spirit." So Jesus must show to them His hands and feet and bid them: "Behold, that it is I myself". "Why are ye troubled," He enquires with some sternness, "and why do thoughts arise in your hearts?" As fear of the Jews kept their doors locked against intrusion, so fear of the supernatural kept their minds closed against the truth. This is a trait impossible and purposeless to invent, but vividly true to everyday experience.

And the same must be said of Luke's penetrating phrase, "they believed not for very joy". This very neatly anticipates the charge of "wishful thinking": it enshrines a wholesome resistance to being misled by what one greatly wishes to believe. The absence of all expectation that Jesus would rise is nowhere more in evidence than in the elaborate preparations for His final burial and the questions debated about rolling away the stone. It is the women who are supposed to be the more easily imposed upon: yet it is they who, though "much perplexed", have as usual the most practical explanation of the empty tomb: "they have taken away the Lord out of the sepulchre". So Mary: "Tell me where thou hast laid him and I will take him hence". This is no hysterical hope of resurrection, but immensely practical, even clinical, commonsense.

The disciples' scornful dismissal of the women's news as "idle tales, and they believed them not", is the understandable, but wholly unworthy, male explanation of the incredible fact! And the two walking to Emmaus pronounce what seems the unanswerable verdict on the women's report: "Him they saw not".

Peter, we are told, departed "wondering"; the rest as yet "knew not the scripture, that he must rise from the dead"; "neither believed they". Even at Christ's final appearance in Galilee, when a much greater number of adherents was present, there still remained "some" who doubted.

Two other details unforgettably emphasise this significant Easter scepticism. One is Thomas' refusal to believe, and the readiness of Jesus to satisfy even his presumptuous conditions

155

of faith. The other, the unexpected sternness of the risen Lord, as He "upbraided them with their unbelief and hardness of heart, because they believed not them which had seen him after he was risen".

Where in all this is the exalted, excited idealism that "expected a resurrection"? Where is the fevered imagination painting a glowing picture of a glorious victory to satisfy messianic faith? To this sceptical mood, exalted, transforming visions do not come, nor do men seeking to impose on the credulity of others confess so freely to sadness, despair, fear, unbelief, astonishment. Of course, faith came eventually, and with it gladness, an intoxicating hope, a boundless joy, an irrepressible enthusiasm, readiness to die rather than deny. But this followed second and third thoughts — the actual moment of transformation from bewilderment to ecstasy is clearly marked: "*then* were the disciples glad when they saw the Lord". But that is the evening of Easter Day, twelve to sixteen hours after Christ had risen.

Here is truth far outstripping possibility of invention: the testimony of various observers, recorded while many eyewitnesses were still alive, without collaboration to deceive (as the variations in detail sufficiently prove), and defended in peril of their lives. The mere existence of these documents, so persuasive, lifelike and sublime, demands an explanation. If Christ be not risen, somewhere in the first century lived history's greatest artist, of incredible skill — and falsehood.

II

Beside this challenging documentary fact stands a second, historical, fact: the existence of the Church. Perhaps the surest evidence of the resurrection of Jesus is the spiritual resurrection of the disciples, the miracle of Christ's continued work.

Out of the disillusioned, despondent, and divided group of heart-sick followers of Jesus was fashioned a social force of such cohesion and impact as to "turn the world upside down", redirect the course of history, and kindle fresh hope in a dying civilisation. G. K. Chesterton described the New Testament Church as "a winged thunderbolt of everlasting enthusiasm"; if Caesar would have phrased the description in less complimentary terms, the violence of Rome's reaction is evidence that she felt the power, and the danger, of this society of saints.

The great historian Harnack, friendly to the faith, traces the Church's effectiveness to her clear message of redemption, fulfilling men's hopes; to the creative moral forces she released in contrast to religion's earlier restrictiveness; to the individualism which made her gospel universal; and to her language of spirit and flesh, life and death, which all could understand. The great Gibbon, on the other side, points to the zeal of primitive Christianity, to the doctrine of immortality, to the miraculous powers, the purer morality, and the steadfast unity, of the Christian society.

Quite so. But what explains the explanations? Whence arose these powerful forces of social regeneration in hearts so humble and unpromising as the defeated eleven in the upper room? Whence came the invincible gladness, the innate authority, that sustained these underprivileged few through empire-wide endeavours against intensest persecution? Whence came to men of narrow Jewish background, who had witnessed Jesus' ignominious death, the profound convictions that shaped their message and their life — the conviction of the universal Lordship of Jesus, the Christ, of His abiding presence with them, and of the world-mission of the Church?

Their own explanation is that they had seen the risen Christ, had heard Him claim such universal Lordship, sending them forth to witness to all nations and promising to be with them to the end of the age. Their lives confirm their words; and the manner of their death, all too often, lent added weight to the testimony of their lives.

Deliberate deception would be motiveless, far too dangerous, and easily discredited; nor could mere fraud sustain the Church for two thousand years of change, hostility, and denial. The cost of Christian fidelity has always been high; its reward too often punishment, imprisonment, and death; its outcome transformed character, purified and *humanised* society, and a proliferation of agencies that have nourished human progress and alleviated innumerable evils. Still the Church is the *only* international society that seeks mankind's redemption; and still she grows — more have joined her ranks in the last century than in any in her history.

If Christ be not raised the existence of His Church is history's outstanding enigma.

III

The ultimate vindication of man's moral judgement and experience is here at stake. If the character, ideals, and vision of Jesus are involved with wholly motiveless deception; if the matchless gospel narratives are products of madness or fraud; if the very fabric of Christian culture, institutions, and hope, and the whole influence of the Church on behalf of education, freedom, womanhood, childhood, healing, peace and truth are founded on a lie, then the moral universe is fundamentally insecure and man's moral "reason" is insane.

Falsehood then becomes more profitable than truth, fraud more fruitful of good than integrity and faithfulness. All moral insight, charity, and hope are undermined, ethical faith is totally discredited, and the world's spiritual resources from which generations of good men and women have drawn their inspiration are finally devalued. Fraud and folly are the saviours of mankind, delusion and deceit the foundations of man's noblest achievement! If Christ be not raised, not only faith but courage, struggle, vision, hope, and ultimately life itself are proved in vain. Then are we lost indeed, without chart or compass in a universe of menace and despair: "of all men most miserable".

But now *is* Christ risen: while conscience, mind, and spiritual experience endure we must reject negation so destructive, suicidal, and morally preposterous. *"Christ is risen . . . .* Be ye therefore steadfast, unmovable, always abounding in the work of the Lord, forasmuch as ye know that your labour is *not* in vain in the Lord."

28 Brave New World Indeed

"Behold, all things are become new. And all things are of God . . . ."   II Corinthians 5:17, 18

OLD DR. MANETTE, in *A Tale of Two Cities,* released after eighteen years' incarceration in the dreaded French Bastille, used still at intervals to relapse into the mental torpor, the vacancy, the endless restless cobbling, which had occupied his long confinement. Living now in a quiet London Square, surrounded with affection, comfort, and friendship, the old man's mind would occasionally return to the fears and fettered loneliness of prison. Actually in a new world of safety, peace, and hope, he lived at such times spiritually in all the gloom and misery of the grim fortress. "Recalled to life", he suffered still, unnecessarily, the pangs of living death.

It is not easy to adjust oneself when the world changes overnight. Peter, Thomas, Mary, and the two of Emmaus walked a new earth with an Easter garden in it and an empty tomb, but they walked with bowed heads and "eyes holden", and with sinking hearts. It is all too easy to profess the Easter faith concerning One "recalled to life" and still to live as in the same old gloomy world between the shadowing doubts of dark Good Friday and the glow of Easter dawn. The failure here is not so much one of faith as of understanding, a failure to appreciate the difference that the resurrection of Jesus has made to *everything*. It is slowness of heart to understand that neither life nor death, things present nor things to come, nor earth nor hell, can ever be the same since Jesus rose again.

I

To live in a world where Jesus is risen is to live in a world where He is our Contemporary. It means that we have not missed Him, after all. We have no need to sing with the children, "I wish that His hands had been placed on my head, that His arms had been thrown around me . . ." for we can know the pressure of His Spirit, the joy of His approving smile, the shadow of His frown:

We may not climb the heavenly steeps
To bring the Lord Christ down;
In vain we search the lowest deeps
For Him no depths can drown.

But warm, sweet, tender, even yet
A present help is He;
And faith has still its Olivet,
And love its Galilee.

The healing of His seamless dress
Is by our beds of pain;
We touch Him in life's throng and press,
And we are whole again.

He is of our age and time, and Christianity is for us essentially what it was for the first Christians long centuries ago — not a school of thought or a branch of culture or a social enthusiasm or the perpetuation of a memory, but a living relationship with a living Lord. It means sitting at His feet in this twentieth century to learn His faith, walking by His side the way He chooses, kneeling in His presence in worship, confession, and prayer, facing up to life and work with His eyes still upon us.

Jesus, the resurrection implies, is never out of date, outdone, or left behind. To live in Him is to live abundantly, to live by Him is to live powerfully, to live with Him is to live joyfully, to live for Him is to live purposefully, to live like Him is to live perfectly. He is not merely yesterday's Hero, or history's Highest Point, but our great Contemporary. He who consistently refused to be confined to Nazareth, to Galilee, to the tomb, refuses to be confined to one long past generation. Our world, this present age, has the living Christ within it, the focal point of Christian faith: for Jesus lives.

II

To live in a world where Jesus is risen is to live in a world where Christ has conquered death. The sure hope of immortality that breathes through the classic literature of devotion, that uplifts the Christian heart in face of sorrow, loneliness, and martyrdom, that sings through our hymnbook and gives eternal horizons to our faith and life, does not rest merely upon universal intuitions, or Scripture promises, or even on the words of Jesus, but upon the abiding fellowship of faithful hearts with Him in every age. It is not argument but spiritual experience which makes eternal life most real. Those to whom "to live is Christ" *know* that death is "gain".

So in the Easter stories all the doors stand open — or are useless. Even the gate of death. Earth is no longer man's prison and grave: it is the antechamber to eternity. A few stoical intellectuals may eloquently persuade themselves that man may base courage to face annihilation upon the foundation of unrelieved despair, not minding much if all his struggle, faith, achievement, science, art, and sacrifice go down at last into eternal nothingness and leave not a wrack behind. The voice of the human heart speaks otherwise — in Auden, for example:

> *crazed we come and coarsened we go*
> *Our wobbling way: there's a white silence*
> *Of antiseptics and instruments*
> *At both ends, but a babble between*
> *And a shame surely. O show us the route*
> *Into hope . . . .*

And the human cry is answered by the angels of the resurrection: "He is risen!" The route into hope runs through a springtime garden past an empty tomb, and He who leads us on is alive forevermore, the focal point of Christian expectation.

III

To live in a world where Jesus is risen is to live in a world where Jesus, and all He stood for, triumphed. This implication of the Easter faith is crucial for a sound moral insight. When Jesus died, the conscience of the race must surely have caught its breath! If that were the end, brute force had triumphed over love, falsehood over truth, evil over righteousness; unscrupulous selfishness wielding material power had conquered faith and faithfulness and innocence.

That such as Jesus could be ultimately defeated, that such a truth be finally denied, such a vision remorselessly exposed, such a cause ruthlessly destroyed, such a faith cruelly disproved, would make of human life a nightmare, and earth a frightening cave of shadows. But Jesus arose. Conscience breathed again. This is a world where Calvary can happen, but in which Calvary is not the end. Back of the seeming triumph of evil are the silent, invincible forces of God: out of every Golgotha that man engineers God accomplishes an Easter Day of victory.

Thus the resurrection of our Lord establishes our faith in the justice of God, in the supremacy of right, in the permanence of things spiritual, in the final adjustment of earth's inequalities and wrong. The mystery of experience becomes intolerable if all beauty, truth, and goodness perish in the grave. The upward striving of the best, man's conquest over nature and patient exploration of the truth, becomes but the dreary procession of misguided dreamers to a silent and eternal darkness: victory remains with short views, selfish aims — the most ruthless, cynical, and vile — unless Jesus arose. But He lives, God's guarantee that, however long the struggle or painful the wounds, right shall triumph, truth outlast deceit, and victory remain with love. The living Christ in an evil world is the focal point of Christian moral confidence.

IV

To live in a world where Jesus is risen is to live in a world where He is still at work. Easter provides a challenging reminder that we stand with the risen Christ at the beginning of an uncompleted story. Beside the ringing cry of the dying Jesus, "It is finished", signalling the accomplishment of the basic work of man's redemption, must be set the last verses of Mark's Gospel where the apostles go forth to proclaim that finished work, "the Lord working with them". And Luke opens the Book of Acts by declaring that the work Jesus had *begun* to do was continued by the Spirit in the Church. For the risen Christ is active yet, sowing the seed of His life and love in succeeding generations. As the whole world is His field, so the whole of history is His working day.

This truth finds impressive illustration in the resurrection records. To every one who saw the empty tomb or met the risen Christ the command was given, in some form or another, to spread the news, to go and tell, to tend the coming flock of those who would believe. The eyes of the risen Jesus were fixed upon the future, and the world with the risen Christ within it is full of worthwhile tasks in which He shares.

For the garden tomb is empty and the East is silver grey
As the angels of the morning trumpet in another day;
See the wounded God go walking down the world's eternal way
For His task is never done.

The living Christ, abroad and active in a needy world, is the focal point of all earth's redeeming energies.

O brave new world, with the risen Jesus in it!

29 Ascension to Pre-eminence

"Lift up your heads, O ye gates; and be ye lift up, ye everlasting doors; and the King of glory shall come in. Who is this King of glory? The Lord strong and mighty, the Lord mighty in battle." Psalm 24:7, 8

WE ARE ALL, far more than we realise, slaves to our imagination. Because Advent, Passiontide, and Easter are associated with vivid pictures and dramatic stories, the message of cradle, cross, and empty tomb is unforgettable. But Ascensiontide lacks such picturesque illustration, and in consequence its glorious truth holds far less place than it deserves in modern Christian thought and life.

Yet the one Ascension picture we possess is memorable. Jesus stands above the assembled disciples on the hillside beyond Bethany, His arms upraised in blessing: as He speaks He is parted from them, taken into glory. That gracious portrait of the Christ of Benediction is surely worthy to stand beside all the treasured cameos of the Master — at Jordan's baptism, in the Nazareth synagogue, moving among the sick, on the Mount of Transfiguration, riding into Jerusalem, in the Garden of Gethsemane, on the cross. The last glimpse given to men of the earthly Jesus is entirely characteristic: grace, power, goodwill, and promise blending in a gesture of blessing and completed in a movement of divine exaltation. That is a scene that should be stamped on every Christian mind.

I

The ascension *fact*, that *Jesus is exalted,* means something more than *Jesus is risen.* Easter affirms that Jesus lives; Ascension, that He is glorified. Easter celebrates His victory over death; Ascension asserts His triumph over all His enemies — and ours.

"When he had by himself purged our sins, he sat down on the right hand of the Majesty on high . . . . Christ is entered into heaven itself, there to appear in the presence of God . . . ever living to make intercession for us." That is the priestly aspect of the Ascension. Christ has passed beyond the veil, to represent us in the eternal sanctuary.

"When he ascended up on high he led a train of captives and distributed gifts unto men . . . . He leads us in the train of his triumph". That is the military view of the Ascension. "The Lord mighty in battle" returns from the arduous campaign magnanimous in victory.

God "hath set him at his own right hand in the heavenly places, far above all principality and power and might and dominion, and every name that is named . . . and hath put all things under his feet". In the thought-world of the Gentile churches of the first century this was the implication of Christ's Ascension that mattered most. Christ is Head over all opposing powers; the kingdom of evil is conquered, and Christ's writ runs in the heavenly places where once the dreaded demons ruled.

Jesus is exalted to be "Lord and Christ" despite the wicked hands which took and slew Him. He is exalted within the Church, given to be "head over all things to the body". He is exalted in the universe, "for by him and for him were all things made, and he is before all things, and by him all things hang together". So Paul saw the exalted Christ on the Damascus road and bowed in utter self-abasement before Him.

"I ascend," said Jesus, "to my Father and to your Father . . . . I go to prepare a place for you". This is the consequence of the Ascension for the Christian hope: Christ is already in the glory, and we depart to be "with Christ, which is far better". There Stephen saw the exalted Christ, *standing* at God's right hand, to receive the saints.

This is the Ascension fact: Jesus is exalted, His apparent failure and defeat eclipsed; "we see Jesus crowned with glory and honour". Men lifted Him upon a cross to die, God raised Him to a throne to rule. There He awaits until His enemies be made His footstool. So John saw Him, the book of the future in His hands, unfolding the destinies of men and nations.

> *Bright portals of the sky,*
> *Embossed with sparkling stars,*
> *Doors of eternity*
> *With diamantine bars,*

Your arras rich uphold,
Loose all your bolts and springs,
Ope wide your leaves of gold
That in your roofs may come the KING OF KINGS!

II

It requires, however, more than a fact to make a festival. The Ascension *fact* generates an Ascension *faith* — in Jesus transcendent. He who had walked amongst men as Brother and Fellow is now lifted far above as King and Lord. And the stupendous truth has two distinct sides.

Jesus, our Fellow and Friend, is beside the eternal throne. That is a great faith in which to face the local magistrate, the provincial Roman governor, or even imperial Caesar; a heartening faith in which to confront the magic, the witchcraft, the curses of paganism; a singing faith in which to dare the malignant spirit-world of evil forces; a glorious faith in which to outface suffering and death.

Far above all that can oppose or threaten, frighten or dismay, Christ is enthroned the Lord, the everlasting King — *and we are His!* And the other side of the Ascension faith is equally uplifting: beside the eternal throne of power and judgement and destiny stands Jesus, our Fellow and Friend, a merciful and faithful High Priest, our Advocate with the Father, the only Mediator between God and man. With the Ascension, the cross gains an immeasurable dimension as the eternal atonement which Jesus offers at the everlasting mercy-seat: "this man, after he had offered one sacrifice for sins for ever, sat down on the right hand of God . . . having obtained eternal redemption for us".

Thus may we "come boldly to the throne of grace, to obtain mercy and find grace to help in time of need", assured that "He is able to save to the uttermost all who come unto God by him, seeing he ever liveth to make intercession for them."

From either point of view the Ascension faith is stimulating and sustaining. We do not think enough of Christ transcendent, raised to be our Representative before God's throne, wearing our manhood in the glory, our Forerunner and File-leader beyond the grave. A cross, and not a crucifix, must be our sign, for while Christ's death must never be forgotten,

He hangs no longer between earth and heaven — our Lord
is in the skies.

> *Humbled for a season,*
> *To receive a name*
> *From the lips of sinners*
> *Unto whom He came,*
> *Faithfully He bore it*
> *Spotless to the last,*
> *Brought it back victorious*
> *When from death He passed;*
>
> *Bore it up triumphant*
> *With its human light,*
> *Through all ranks of creatures,*
> *To the central height;*
> *To the throne of Godhead,*
> *To the Father's breast,*
> *Filled it with glory*
> *Of that perfect rest.*

III

Yet even Ascension fact plus Ascension faith do not make a
Christian life; the Ascension ideal is as important as either.
"God hath given him a name that is above every name that
at the name of Jesus *every knee should bow*". He is Head
of the Church, Lord of creation, exalted to God's right hand,
"that in all things he might have the pre-eminence".

Here the festival of the Ascension bears directly upon the
Christian's daily behaviour. The issue is in part one of
deliberate priorities, of giving to Christ absolute pre-eminence
in all our loyalties. He is the first and last in Christian
hearts, with the right to command and authority to dispose,
claiming precedence, if need arise, over love of parent, wife,
or child, and always over love of wealth, ease, safety, and life
itself. Pre-eminent in character, suffering, love, and sacrifice,
He has justified His claim to be pre-eminent in the hearts of
those who follow Him; by His exaltation to God's side that
claim is forever established by divine decree.

Hereby we may discover where we stand in spiritual matu-
rity. We begin with Jesus in the lowly manger in gentleness
and beauty, and perhaps imagine we are doing well religiously
if a Christmas kindliness suffuse our hearts. We think of

Jesus ministering in Galilee, and suppose that we are Christians if occasionally we help our fellows. Sometimes perhaps we are reminded of His death, and try sincerely to feel grateful. But the crucial understanding comes as we lift our eyes to Jesus exalted, transcendent, glorified, claiming from us the foremost place, the topmost priority, the furthermost loyalty, the uttermost love. By our reaction to that demand we know just where we are.

But the practical issue of the Ascension is also in part a matter of orientation, the conscious direction of the soul's gaze and aim towards an ascended Lord. "If ye then be risen with Christ, seek those things which are above, where Christ sitteth on the right hand of God. Set your affection on things above, not on things on the earth. For ye are dead, and your life is hid with Christ in God. When Christ, who is our life, shall appear, then shall ye also appear with him in glory".

Into this one glowing passage are gathered the inner life's up-stretching ambition ("seek ye"), its disciplined desire ("set your affection"), its secret resources ("life hid with Christ in God"), its final hope ("when Christ shall appear"), and its ultimate goal ("ye shall appear with him in glory"), and all is set in the light of the Ascension ("above, where Christ sitteth"). A soul so fixed upon the transcendent Christ will have no perplexity or hesitation about its spiritual priorities. The ascended Lord claims the ascendancy: clearly seen, and truly worshipped, He cannot but be pre-eminent — in all things.

30 The Great Commission

*"All power is given unto me in heaven and in earth. Go ye
therefore, and teach all nations, baptising them . . . teaching
them to observe all things whatsoever I have commanded
you: and, lo, I am with you alway, even unto the end of
the world."*   Matthew 28:18-20

A WONDERFUL OUTREACH of faith, expansiveness of vision, and
amplitude of life marks the Church of the New Testament.
Apostolic Christianity possessed almost a fourth dimension:
it was no limited, niggardly "thing done in a corner", the
hobby of certain "types", the occupation of idle moments, the
product of passing moods. It was all-inclusive — in scope, in
purpose, in demand, and in invitation. It encircled life and
circumnavigated experience: it continually envisaged and
wholeheartedly embraced "all things".

"He that spared not his own Son . . . how shall he not with
him also freely give us *all things? All things* work together
for good . . . *all things* are yours . . . in *all things* more than
conquerors . . . He hath given us *all things* that pertain to
life and godliness . . . . *All things* are of God . . . . Christ is
head over *all things* to the church . . . that in *all things* he
might have the pre-eminence . . . . He is before *all things,* and
by Him all things cohere . . . . I can do *all things* through
Christ . . . able to subdue *all things* unto himself . . . God
hath put *all things* under his feet."

This can be no mere trick of speech, or thoughtless exaggeration. It is the superabounding faith of men who affirm
their confidence that to the man of God all things are
possible to him that believeth. But whence came this wide-
ranging assurance, this limitless confidence in the fullness of
the blessing of the gospel? Might it not derive from the
Church's first commission spoken directly to the apostles by
the ascending Lord — "All power is given unto me . . . teach
all nations . . . observe all things . . . . And, lo, I am with you
all the days"?

169

I

Here at any rate the apostles learned the hidden depths of the Church's spiritual resources: "All *power* is given unto me . . . go ye therefore". No age has been more obsessed than ours with the secrets, the necessity, the psychology of power. The mighty bang, the irresistible thrust, a blasting heat or furious speed; the political coup, the block vote, ruthlessness, great numbers — these are the modern symbols of power. In them, we assume, lies the dynamic that gets things done. And because the Church possesses none of them we suppose her powerless. Judging by foolhardy standards we are depressed by wholly unsound and unworthy conclusions.

History falsifies our estimate. Beyond question, the things that have really shaped humanity's experience and still determine her destiny are of another kind. *Truth,* for example, that silently counters error, pierces arrogance, exposes folly, bores irresistibly into the soul of a generation and inflames the conscience of an age. *Ideas* that have legs and arms, fascination and energy — ideas like freedom, equality, peace, God. *Goodness,* too, that quenches the flame of revenge, kindles the love of honourable men, lingers in beneficent influence to the third and fourth generations, and gives birth to countless merciful reforms. *Courage,* again, can shape the destiny of a time, preserving integrity, fulfilling its vows, resisting evil at great cost. *Faith* has accomplished, endured, destroyed, rebuilt, preserved, outlasted, dared, and created more things in heaven and earth than are recorded in time's registers. *Hero-worship* — the infection of greatness — at once inspires, rebukes and redeems, and binds individuals together into compact societies that are the real pressure-groups of history. And *love,* which none can usefully analyse or imitate, or live worthily without.

Here is power. These are the forces embedded in the moral universe awaiting discovery and application as surely as magnetism and nuclear energy awaited discovery and application in the physical world. These are the vibrant currents of the energies of God playing over human lives: and "All are mine" says Jesus — all power in heaven and earth that moves men's minds, stabs awake the sleeping conscience, pursues the rebellious, woos the impenitent, fashions character, directs history, and determines destiny — "All power is given unto me".

"And, lo, I am with you." Such are the Church's spiritual resources, awaiting to be tapped by prayer, liberated in devotion, utilised in service, harnessed by efficient consecration, impressed upon society in a fine tradition of great souls and a zealous organisation of good works. The Church is far indeed from being powerless: within her stands the Christ, "the power of God".

II

On the mount of the Ascension the assembled disciples, seeing the King in His beauty saw also "the land of far distances" and learned from the ascending Lord the immense breadth of the Church's appointed horizons. Her field is to be "all the nations".

Geographically, of course, that means the world, and in the twentieth century the logic of that commission is inescapable. Whatever previous generations may have thought, we know that the kind of world we want must be conceived as *one* world; and we know that the kind of world-order we desire must have spiritual foundations. It follows that the hope of mankind lies in the Christian missionary cause, the deliberate extension of Christian witness and enterprise to the ends of the earth.

Socially, the commission to all nations directs Christian attention and concern towards all sorts and conditions of men. "We are debtors," says Paul, the university man, the rabbi, "to the barbarian" as well as to the Greek; to the uneducated and the dull as well as to the wise, to the slave as well as to his master. The moral implications of a universal gospel must not be evaded: a broad intellectual horizon demands a large heart.

Individually, the commission to the world includes the young, the middle-aged, the old, the influential, and the underprivileged, men and women in the mass, and the man, the woman, alone. With the story of Jesus before us we know it means especially the last: "to every single creature". Sometimes the horizon of Christian concern can be set so wide and distant that the lonely individual gets overlooked against the background of his "class" and "social problem". It was never so with Christ.

Not easily, or quickly, did the apostolic Church rise to the height of her great charge to carry her gospel to all mankind, nor are we always ready to translate the vision and the words into gifts and enterprise. Yet such is the great commission: and we limit the scope of the appointed target only at the peril of deliberate disobedience, and to our own serious impoverishment.

III

"Baptising them . . . teaching them to observe all things whatsoever I have commanded you": so the apostles learned from their ascending Lord the towering height of the Church's task. It is hard to make some people realise that the Church of Christ is not free to revise her programme, to reword her message, in order to accommodate every change in intellectual climate, every veering alternation of popular fancy. Her work is prescribed for her with unambiguous clarity: "teach all things whatsoever I command". That is the least, and the most, she has to say.

Two elements of that charge may be remarked. Baptism witnesses to conversion; it declares, as the threefold Name implies, the Christian's faith in the Father, love of the Son, acceptance of the Holy Spirit. Here Christian life begins, and to the necessity for such new beginnings the Church must faithfully bear witness. That they are possible, through Christ, even for the worst, is the glad good news she brings to men.

The other noticeable feature of the charge is the word "commanded". Much of faith and theology is implicit in every word of Christ, but as the Gospels show, the emphasis of His counsel is ever upon behaviour — upon what a man *does* because he so *believes*. So the Church must work to bring men not merely to right thinking and orthodoxy of belief, but — keeping the Master's emphasis — to the quality of living appropriate to the children of the King.

Meticulous loyalty to Christ's sayings would lend a totally new relevance to the Church's message in our time. Jesus said many pertinent and disturbing things about love of riches, and spiritual bankruptcy; about one's attitude to enemies; about ostentatious religiousness; about the enjoyment of lust; about aggressiveness, and peacemaking; about the psychiatrist's ideal of purity of heart; about caring for the underfed, the sick, the friendless, and the refugee; about the kingdom of spiritual values that judges and devalues the world's prized goals; about prayer; about God and the dethroned self. Whenever the Church observes the command to teach what the Master said, she speaks with exceptional authority and directness to the modern situation.

IV

No less surely the apostles derived from the ascending Lord their unbounded confidence in the Church's final perseverance. As Jesus had said at Caesarea, that the gates of hell should not prevail against His Church, so here at Bethany He promises to be with her to the end of time.

It is difficult now to believe that the Church's very survival seemed in doubt on that Ascension Day, as these disciples faced Jewry's hostility, and behind that, Caesar's might. But if any questioned the future, the answer surely lay in the promise that He, to whom belongs all power, would be beside them to the consummation of the age.

This is the supreme miracle of the Church's story — her simple preservation. In years of ignominy and oppression she outfaced and outlived the ancient pagan world. In generations of persecution she outfought and outlasted the mighty Roman empire. In times of unbelief and heresy she outthought and outwitted the enemies of faith. In the dark ages of betrayal and decay she outmanoeuvred the forces of superstition and corruption. In a century of narrowing nationalism her missionary zeal outreached to lands of primitive and militant heathenism, and outmatched the attendant perils and reprisals with courage, endurance, and love.

This is the "nourishing and cherishing" which Paul says illustrates the love of Jesus for His church, and it is evidence enough that through the long centuries the ascended Lord has faithfully kept His word. He is with her, always, and in power.

Such a Church, empowered, universal, commissioned, and

indestructible, is the legacy of Christ to history and to ourselves. Within her fellowship our own individual discipleship is enriched. By her worship and witness our own faith is instructed, nourished, and enlarged. Through her corporate work our own service of Christ's Kingdom is enhanced and sanctified. Between the far-off days in Galilee and our much troubled, tangled time there stretches this living bridge of saints, the Church militant and triumphant. As in our turn we take our place in the lengthening roll of those who through good report and ill have followed Christ, we know that He is with us yet, Stranger of Galilee, and yet best known, best loved of all earth's heroes, Friend of sinners, and Saviour of the world.

friendship. Conscious of immaculate purity, He moves with understanding and forgiving pity among the stained and fallen. No element of moral worth is missing from His mind and heart: and the varied vibrant tones of His rich nature blend in a symphony of consistent beauty and balanced power beside which all other lives seem partial and discordant.

Impressive illustration of this wholeness of Christ's character is found in His unique power to attract men of all races. It is difficult to imagine Gautama, Mahomet, Confucius, or even Socrates, awakening equal devotion in Scandinavia, North America, India, the Congo forest, around the Mediterranean, and among South Sea Islanders, American Indians, Slav, Teuton, Japanese and Anglo-Saxon. Yet this Jesus certainly has done.

Even where outright conversion is rare, Christ's ethical ideal and personal greatness are readily approved. Jesus has been accepted into the Hindu pantheon; He is respected in Islam; every new religious sect pays some degree of lip-service to His pre-eminence. When Chinese and Indian object to Christianity as a "Western" religion, and Bible students of the West struggle with the mental adjustments necessary for interpreting an essentially oriental literature, one realises how completely "the Galilean Jew" — whose ultimate family roots lie deep in Mesopotamia — has transcended the racial and ethnic divisions of mankind by a quality of humanity universally understood, admired, and approved.

The prevailing impression of Jesus upon modern minds concerns His meekness and patience, His gentleness, peaceableness, and love. Innumerable sayings and deeds among the neediest folk verify this partial portrait. When, keeping these in mind, we also recall His undaunted courage, unflinching challenge, heroic endurance, sharp anger, unhesitating exposure of falsehood, bracing sternness, uncompromising realism, and unlimited demand; His strong selflessness, His healthy outward-looking soul, and His fearless acceptance of the cross, we begin to grasp the comprehensiveness, the architectural balance and proportion of Christ's incomparable character.

> His life was gentle, and the elements
> So mixed in him that nature might stand up
> And say to all the world, "This was a man!"

Assessments that demand response

The Master of men

The Son of God

The Lord of life

The Spirit of Christ

The coming King

31 The Master of Men

"Behold the man!"

PILATE'S EXHORTATION to the Jerusalem crowd, "
man", was probably no more than an appeal to
for the bound, scourged, bleeding, thorn-crowne
Jesus. But his words provide a striking, if accider
to a demand heard oftener in the ancient wor
our own.

Diogenes is said to have once scoured Athens day
with a lantern, ostentatiously searching for a
Jeremiah was charged to

> Run to and fro through the streets of Jeru
> Look, and take note!
> Search her squares to see
> If you can find a man —
> One who does justice and seeks truth.

Cynic and prophet agree on the importance of
quality; alike they have learned that in the last reso
institutions, laws, traditions, nor culture can preser
or initiate new good if men of principle, vision, va
truth cannot be found.

i

Assessment of Jesus may therefore well begin wit
unconsciously significant tribute: "Behold the *ma*
is manhood in its noblest expression, its peerless b
ming in itself all the varieties of goodness and perso
that our hearts instinctively admire.

Jesus is strong as the sternest of commanders, ye
as any woman. He has wealth of power and immense
tration of will, yet He is too sympathetic, too gentle,
the bruised reed of a penitent heart or quench the g
flax of a weak faith. He is so dynamic that He sets
world-movements, so majestic and authoritative in act
speech that none dare openly oppose, yet He sits w
among children, and the poor in spirit find comfort

II

Perfection of character lies, however, not alone in inherent qualities, but also in positive, outreaching, and creative influence: and here the matchless manhood of the Master proves its power. Jesus is essentially a *maker* of men.

Sometimes we see the recreating process going on slowly, as in the gradual change of the coarse, swearing, violent yet cowardly Simon into the fearless and tender apostle Peter. Sometimes the work is condensed into sudden but complete conversion, as the dishonest, avaricious Zaccheus becomes in a moment just and generous. Sometimes the process is wholly hidden, and we see only the finished result in purified womanhood and restored self-respect. Sometimes again part of the process is visible, part simply miraculous and inexplicable, as when the proud, self-righteous, intensely nationalistic Saul is transformed into a humble, chastened, winsome missionary with the whole world in his heart. The method matters little: in each case we are witnessing the most amazing miracle of all, the remaking of men.

Surprisingly enough in this age of psychology and humanism, the very possibility of such remoulding of humanity's broken earthenware into serviceable vessels for society and for God is frequently denied. A man is, we are told, what the past has made him, whether his own yesterday, or the dimly remembered events of his childhood, or the unconscious but powerful hangover of heredity, or the long-range, irresistible forces of the racial subconscious, accumulated in the long painful climb from primeval mud to the space-probing missile. And since the past is unalterable, man is unchangeable. Economic man, evolutionary man, social man, scientific man — whatever the epithet, the pessimism remains. An amoral "realism" wedded to materialist science can find no hope for the rehabilitation of the vicious, the selfish, the truly wicked, or for the self-destructive elements in civilisation. Even the psychological imitations of religious techniques fail to work, until the patient becomes convinced that the religion is *true*.

Then the miracle happens. Man, we discover, is made what he is not by the past alone but by the expected, desired, and sought-for future: by the ideal ahead and the spiritual forces within and the accessible God above, and by all these as focussed in Christ, the Redeemer and Saviour and Remaker of souls. In the forgiveness He speaks, and the love He kindles, and the faith He imparts that better is possible; even the influence of the past becomes transformed from burden to spur: "if any man be in Christ he is a new creature; old things are passed away; behold all things are become new." If any man be in Christ, he is a new made man.

And what men He makes! Paul, Augustine, Luther, Carey, Wesley, Livingstone, Damien, Kagawa, Sundar Singh, and their kind are among the truly strong, the really great; while beside them march a host of countless unremembered men and women who in their day were the salt of the earth, the foundation of social good, the hope of the world's future.

It little avails that Jesus be the matchless Man if this be not also true: that under His influence and in His company and by His hands men are re-made. But it is gloriously true. The making of men is His prerogative, and His delight.

III

Much, then, is suggested in the title men gave to Jesus, and which He accepted, in the days of His flesh — the significant name of "Master". Such a word implies both His abiding superiority in the things that make for manhood, and the technique of His saving, redeeming work.

Jesus *remains* the greatest the world has ever seen. His teaching still penetrates the heart of all vital truth, soars above all other ideals and hopes and moral endeavour. The world has not outlived His message, or bettered His vision, or outdated His story. We can point to none whose life is purer, more significant, more perfect, more relevant to the appalling predicament of mankind. We have failed to follow, even occasionally have failed to understand Him. But we have not excelled His standard, or conceived anyone or anything that can. He is still the Master.

Nor can His method be improved. He transforms men by *mastering* them from within: and our disordered human nature needs nothing so desperately as someone or something to reduce our inner conflicts to order and peace, to harness the warring elements of a personality half-animal half-angel to some sublime, subduing purpose.

In our generation we have learned to our cost what power is released when one man is given control of the bodies and souls of his fellows. What might have been achieved if Jesus had the same unquestioning obedience! But the mastery Christ exercises is leadership through love, not dictatorship through fear. He calls, pleads, and invites men to surrender; by the perfection of His own life He establishes His moral right to show us how to live; His costly service of our need forges between our hearts and His a bond of grateful love. Because of all He was, and did, to be His bondslaves is our perfect freedom; His redeeming mastery of us becomes our only hope of liberty and joy.

IV

These are vast claims to make, and they bring us but to the threshold of understanding who He is. Even so, the claims are subject to personal confirmation. This matchless Master and Remaker of men offers to remake *us*. The only adequate response to such a claim, if we are truly in earnest in seeking the truth, is to let Him do so.

Read and re-read the story for yourself. Make His teaching your rule of life — say for three years. Live as in His company, make His example your pattern, conduct your affairs so as to satisfy His standards, and aim in all things to win His approval. There is no doubt of the result. Soon, very soon, you will learn your need of His help and grace; soon you will realise He far exceeds all merely human categories. He will prove Himself alive, helpful, gracious, and divine. Give Him but opportunity in *your* life and He will amply vindicate His claim to be: the Master of men.

32 The Son of God

"The Son of God is come."
"God was in Christ."
"Truly this man was a son of God."

I John 5:20, II Corinthians 5:19, Mark 15:39

MODERN FOLK commonly have little patience with the long controversies that in earlier centuries rent the Church concerning the Person of her Lord. The literary deposit of those endless arguments in the longer Christian creeds is scarcely intelligible nowadays, and the whole tone and language of the various contending parties seem to us infinitely remote from the teaching of Jesus and the "simple faith" of apostolic Christians.

This attitude is understandable; but it is very superficial. It ignores what is perhaps the oddest of all facts about the first records of the life of Jesus: the fact, namely, that one after the other they labour to emphasise that Christ *was man*.

I

The earliest portrait of Jesus — that of Mark — presents innumerable features designed to leave no doubt that He was truly man. Mark shows Him sometimes angry, questioning, and weary; sometimes disobeyed, derided, scorned, and slandered; occasionally displeased, and even frustrated by the actions and the unbelief of others. His approaching passion repeatedly weighed upon His spirit. He confessed ignorance of the Last Day, and the scene in Gethsemane is dwelt upon with especial poignancy. From very early in Mark's story, hostility and threats gather about Christ's head, and He is shown to be intimately involved alike in the sufferings and in the evil conspiracies of sinful hearts. Yet Mark explicitly declares that he is writing the good news of the Son of God.

The gospel record most concerned with the divinity of Christ begins with the uncompromising statement that He was "made flesh", and from that point onwards loses no opportunity to underline the humanity of Christ. Jesus shares a simple marriage feast, understands what is in man, grows weary with journeying, loves deeply the Bethany family, grieves at the death of a friend, is much moved by the affectionate love of Mary, and "troubled" on His arrival at the capital. He is so lowly among men as to wash the disciples' feet, so fully man as to seek in prayer the inward resources for His passion. And John's Gospel, more than any other, makes us enter feelingly into all the human horror of Christ's death.

The Epistle to the Hebrews is no less emphatic that Jesus took upon Him the nature of man, was made a little lower than the angels, was sharply tempted, prayed "with strong crying and tears", learned obedience by the things which He endured, being made perfect through suffering, and finally tasting death for every man. Jesus is the leader of all who live by faith, and not ashamed to call them brethren; indeed, it is because He was "chosen from among men" that He is able to be a faithful High Priest for humanity. Yet is He most certainly God's Son, whose throne is "for ever and ever".

The First Epistle of John roundly declares that anyone who denies that Christ has come in human flesh is "not of God".

It is surely strange that such a fact should need to be underlined at all. Yet the apostolic faith in Christ, worship of Christ, consecration to Christ, preaching of Christ, prayer to Christ, all rest without hesitation or argument upon the certainty that He was divine. Just because they were so sure of that, the other truth, that He took the form of a servant and was made in the likeness of men, needed to be carefully safeguarded. Concerning no other figure in human history does this necessity arise: but of Jesus it was theologically and religiously imperative to allow no doubt that He was man.

II

This odd concern is, of course, only the highest expression and consequence of the strangeness that lingers about the gospel portrait of Jesus, the persistent impression that He is not wholly of this world, that in the division between human and divine He belongs on the far side of the gulf — that in fact He is man *by choice,* and not as we are.

This impression is prepared for by many details in His story. The peerless perfection of His character, the self-evident authority of His truth, the creative and redemptive power of His influence, the miracle of His sinlessness, and the crowning marvel of His resurrection all imply that ordinary human categories of greatness will not suffice for Jesus. The record of the Church and personal experience of His saving grace in our own lives leave no shadow of doubt as to the divine source of His being and salvation.

It is however from His own lips that the conclusive evidence is heard. Not only does Christ declare that His presence among men is the crucial moment of responsibility for mankind; not only does He speak with unshakable assurance of Himself as the source of man's salvation, the way, truth, and life that man desperately needs, the judge of souls and the light of the world. He does not merely speak authoritative pardon, and equally authoritative warning, in God's name, and make promises concerning the Spirit, concerning prayer, concerning immortality, which only divine authority could justify. Besides all this, the Master takes upon His lips explicit words that from anyone else would make us shudder.

"No man knoweth the Son, save the Father, and no man knoweth the Father save the Son, and he to whomsoever the Son willeth to reveal him . . . . Last of all, God sent his Son . . . . All power is given unto me in heaven and in earth . . . . The Father hath committed all judgement unto the Son . . . . I and the Father are one . . . . He that hath seen me hath seen the Father . . . . No man cometh unto the Father but by me."

Such sayings cannot be evaded. Here our assessment of Jesus is decisive. "Either He is God, or He is neither good nor sane" may seem a crude statement of the issue, but something very like it constitutes the dilemma with which we are faced. If Jesus is wrong about Himself, He cannot be trusted about anything.

The apostolic Church was sure He was not wrong. Language becomes strained, metaphors multiply, as Christian leaders strive to express their thought about Jesus: "In the

form of God . . . equality with God . . . . Declared to be
the Son of God . . . . By whom he made the worlds . . . . In
Him dwelleth all the fulness of the Godhead . . . . The
outshining of God's glory and the express image of his
person . . . . The Son, heir of all things . . . . The Word
who was with God from the beginning, and who was God,
who became flesh . . . . The Son who came from God and
went to God . . . . The Lord from heaven".

Nor has the later Church been persuaded to revise this
supreme assessment of the person of her Lord. All Christian
experience has confirmed what our Lord's own words, apostolic Scripture, and Christian philosophy require, that "God
was in Christ". In Him the unfathomable ocean of Deity
washes humanity's shores. That is the final Christian judgement about Jesus — and the heart of the Christian gospel:
"God so loved the world that he gave his only begotten
Son . . . . The Father sent the Son to be the saviour of
the world".

III

And so we return once more to experience, to the gospel,
and the salvation of the world. To assume that all such
declarations about the Son of God are "mere theology",
remote from Christian living, is to misread entirely both the
New Testament and the Christian life. It is also to miss a
fascinating characteristic of the gospel records. For in the
Gospels every reference to Jesus' eternal Sonship is related
immediately to His redemptive task.

In Matthew 11, the unique relation of Jesus to the Father
("No man knoweth the Son save the Father . . . the Father
save the Son . . .") is linked at once to the glorious invitation:
"Come unto me all ye that labour and are heavy laden, and
I will give you rest". Just because He is the divine Son and
able fully to reveal the Father, He can offer freely that rest
in God which is perfect refreshment and ultimate peace.

In John 13 the unparalleled Sonship of Jesus as the One
into whose hands the Father has committed all things and
who came from God is linked directly to the most sublime
example of the Christian ethic in Christ's washing of the
disciples' feet. For only the plenary grace of a divine

Christ can make the Christian law of self-abasing love a practicable precept for human nature.

In Matthew 28 Jesus' possession of all power in heaven and in earth and His personal continuance with the Church to the end of the age are related immediately to the great commission laid upon the Church to make disciples of all nations. Only so great a Christ can equip the Church for what she has to do; only under a divine Lord does her world-embracing task seem possible, or her triumph in a sinful, hostile world become conceivable.

And in John 6, when the crowd turned from Jesus in Galilee, and He wistfully asked the Twelve, "Will ye also go away?" the reply of Peter is clear: "Lord, to whom shall we go? Thou hast the words of eternal life. And we believe and are sure that thou art that Christ, the Son of the living God." For once again it is the fact of His divine Sonship which imparts life to His words, and salvation to all who believe on Him.

The gospel's gracious invitation, superb example, far-reaching commission, and full salvation all rest thus directly upon Christ's sufficiency, as the eternal Son of the ever living God. "Of his fulness have all we received, grace upon grace." The divinity of Christ and the richness of Christian experience and hope are inextricably related; in the deepest sense they are two aspects of the same great truth, that "God was in Christ".

IV

"Show us the Father" is Philip's profound expression of the deep hunger behind the whole religious quest, speaking for saints and mystics, thinkers, moralists, and men of faith of every age. "He that hath seen me hath seen the Father" is Christ's staggering reply. That is what the doctrine of Christ's divine Sonship really means, and why it matters. In His words we hear God speaking; in His deeds we see God at work; in His reproach we glimpse God's judgement; in His love we feel God's heart beating. If this be not true, we know nothing of God at all. If it be true — and we know it is — then God is like Jesus, and Jesus is God manifest in the flesh, the unique, incomparable, only begotten Son of the ever-living God.

> *None other Lamb, none other Name,*
> *None other hope in heaven or earth or sea,*
> *None other hiding place from guilt and shame —*
> *None beside Thee.*

33 The Lord of Life

"Ye call me Master and Lord: and ye say well; for so I am."
John 13:13

THE ESSENCE OF Christian worship, the earliest Christian creed, the simplest Christian ethic, the Church's universal standard of membership, are all summed up in one primitive Christian watchword: "Jesus is Lord". Whether in Hebrew dress, as "Jesus [is] Christ", or in the more theological phrase, "Jesus the Son of God"; in the common Gentile term "Jesus is Lord" or the less formal "Master", the meaning of the ascription is ever the same: it is the acknowledgement of Christ's absolute authority over the lives of those who profess His name. The Lordship of Christ is the focal centre of apostolic Christianity.

I

This is so important as to demand detailed illustration. That "Jesus is Lord" is the all-significant announcement which transformed the common knowledge about Jesus' life into a saving and divisive message: "God hath made this same Jesus . . . both Lord and Christ". "We preach . . . Christ Jesus the Lord" is the constant note of Paul's preaching; and Peter's work is defined as "preaching good news of peace by Jesus Christ — he is Lord of all". "Jesus is the Christ" is the earliest formulation of the Church's "foundation faith" by Peter at Caesarea Philippi, and it remains the confession required of converts: "If thou shalt confess with thy mouth Jesus as Lord . . .". Into His name as Lord were new believers baptised, usually upon some such confession as that of the eunuch: "I believe that Jesus Christ is the Son of God".

Similarly, confession of Christ's Lordship becomes the simple but sufficient test of sincere worship: "No man can say Jesus is Lord, but by the Holy Ghost", Paul counsels the disorderly worshippers at Corinth. It is likewise the test of spiritual experience: "Whosoever shall confess that Jesus is the Son of God, God dwelleth in him and he in God"; and also of spiritual victory: "Who is he that overcometh . . . but he that believeth that Jesus is the Son of God?"

"Ye call me Master and Lord," said Jesus, "and ye say well, for so I am." "For this purpose," echoes Peter, "Jesus both died and rose again, that he might be Lord." "God hath highly exalted him, that at the name of Jesus every knee should bow and every tongue confess that Jesus is Lord." At the centre of the Church's life stands the table of the Lord, with the cup of the Lord showing the Lord's death; the routine of the Church's worship moves around the Lord's day; the controlling aim of the individual Christian life is to "do all in the name of the Lord Jesus"; and the essence of the Christian hope is Maranatha — Lord, come!

Thus we may say with fairness that as "Son of God" expresses the final Christian judgement about the person of Jesus, so "Jesus is Lord" enshrines the fundamental Christian attitude towards Him. This is, so to speak, the practical and moral aspect of our assessment of the Stranger of Galilee. That Jesus is Lord sums up the meaning of His earthly story, expresses the response of grateful hearts towards His sacrifice, and embodies a practical faith in His deathless life and rightful, glorious exaltation. Confronted with Jesus, the heart's only adequate reaction is that of Saul of Tarsus: "Lord, what wilt thou have me to do?"

II

It is scarcely possible at this date to hear this familiar title for Jesus with anything of the feeling, or the sense of shock, with which it was first used. To Romans, born and trained to the imperial manner, with a profound sense of the state's absolute power and an even profounder awe of "divine Caesar", the name "Lord" belonged to one only in all the world — to the wearer of the imperial purple and the wielder of imperial might. To give Caesar's proud title to the Carpenter of Nazareth was ridiculous — or frightening.

The young soldier standing in the barracks, or before the magistrate, to confess that Jesus was his Caesar risked everything for Christ. The word's perilous political ring echoes in the contemptuous accusation flung against Paul and Silas — "They preach another king, one Jesus"; its exasperating implications can still startle us in the magistrate's demand of Polycarp — "What harm is there in saying 'Caesar is Lord'?".

To the Jew the title's assumptions were even more daring. Brought up in the synagogues of the Dispersion to hear the Greek Bible read, and to say his prayers in the Greek language, he would know the word "Lord" as the regular, familiar name for God. In Judaist ears, "Jesus is Lord" was either the most astonishing good news or sheer blasphemy, punishable with death.

The superstitious Gentile found the title scarcely less significant. The gods many and lords many of pagan religion, the Lord Serapis, the Lord Mithras, and many others, represented a host of principalities and powers, thrones, dominions, and lordships in whose hands lay all man's welfare, fate, and destiny. To call Jesus, alone, Lord was to claim for Him a dominion beyond the realms of space and time; and for oneself, a glorious liberation from fear and bondage to malignant and unclean domination.

For the slave, once more, the man without rights, possessions, or protection, to call Jesus Lord was to acknowledge at once the utmost bondage human hearts can know, and the fullest freedom. "Jesus is Lord" meant to the slave-owner that even masters have their Master in heaven; to his chattels it meant that even the poor slave was the Lord's freedman.

Each of these meanings of the word is written into first-century literature; each touched intimately the living experience of the first Christians. It was precisely, and deliberately, against this political background of Caesar-worship, this theological background of the Jewish Scriptures, this popular background of demonic superstition, this social background of slavery, that the Church dared to frame her good news, her high faith, her fearless challenge, and her undying hope in the provocative watchword: "Jesus is Lord".

III

The affirmative form of this declaration of faith and obedience could not hide the fact that it necessarily involved the equally deliberate, and costly, *denial* of the supremacy of the state, of the finality of the Old Testament, of the power of the demons, of the subservience of the soul to any man. The perils linked to such a confession ensured therefore in the earliest days that mere lip-service to Christ's Lordship would rarely pass for sincere profession. But the temptation to take words for deeds was always present; in easier times profession could become the substitute for consecration. And so the Church preserved faithfully some searching words of Jesus which warn against mere orthodoxy of language.

"Why call ye me Lord, Lord, and do not the things that I say? Not every one that saith unto me, Lord, Lord, shall enter into the kingdom of heaven, but he that doeth the will of my Father which is in heaven. Many will say to me in that day, Lord, Lord, have we not prophesied in thy name, and in thy name have cast out devils, and in thy name done many wonderful works? And then will I profess unto them, I never knew you . . . . "

Thus by the practice of obedience which it implied, as well as by the persecution it provoked, the Christian confession was kept true and meaningful. Every *thought* was to be brought into captivity to the obedience of Christ. As they had received Christ Jesus "as Lord", so were they to *"walk in him"*. All their activity in the Church was to be "worthy of the Lord"; they were to be fervent in spirit as men "serving the Lord"; their daily work must be done as "unto the Lord". Their very bodies were "the Lord's", and must be preserved unto Him; so marriage was to be "only in the Lord". All was planned and done "if the Lord will"; they lived "unto the Lord" and they died "unto the Lord"; whether they lived or died they were "the Lord's". Certainly they filled the title with significance by the way they lived, and lent to the confession power by the price they paid for loyalty.

IV

To Christian hearts Jesus is much else beside Lord and Master: He is Saviour, Redeemer, Companion, and Friend. But it remains true that He is nothing at all to us unless He is *also* Lord. The love of God affords no comfort, the gospel no hope, the presence of God brings no joy, the grace of God no salvation to hearts that refuse His claim and resist His rule.

191

And He *deserves* to rule. Like some snow-capped Alpine peak aloof and awe-inspiring, nearer to heaven than to earth, Jesus towers above the plain of our common humanity: above us in His quality of manhood, above us in His sinlessness, above us in the fulness of divine power that flowed through Him, above us in the authority of His thought and claims and deeds, above us in the grace that suffered and died for our sakes — solitary, incomparable, in His resurrection from the dead, without peer and beyond praise as Son of the living God. He bears the thorn-crown and the reed-sceptre and wears the stained mocking purple as insignia of a greater empire than Caesar could dream or the world has ever known. *Jesus is Lord* — King of kings and Lord of lords:

> *All hail the power of Jesus' name!*
> *Let angels prostrate fall:*
> *Bring forth the royal diadem*
> *And crown Him Lord of all.*
>
> *Oh, that with yonder sacred throng*
> *We at His feet may fall,*
> *Join in the everlasting song*
> *And crown Him, Lord of all.*

34 *The Spirit of Christ*

*"It is expedient for you that I go away: for if I go not away,
the Comforter will not come unto you; but if I depart, I
will send him unto you."*   John 16:7

VERY FEW FOUNDERS of great movements or pioneers of thought
or action can have dared to say to those who followed them:
"It is expedient for you that I go away". The problem of
perpetuating any new work in the world, any novel teaching
or example, when the original impetus has gone, is rarely
solved. Many methods have been tried, with but indifferent
success. On the whole it might be said that mankind has
been more proficient at breaking new ground than at preserving the treasure therein discovered — and it needs both
abilities to enrich the world.

I

Buddha, it was believed, enshrined his thought in an oral,
memorised tradition of doctrine. But the idolatry he opposed
soon compromised the teaching, and Buddhism today is
very different from the message of the Buddha. Jesus left
no oral system of thought, only scattered memories of the
kind of things He said, to be patiently gathered together by
the gospel writers in after years. The truth is that Christ's
message and meaning are too rich to be captured in any form
of words.

Mahomet tried a written record, on the Jewish model,
preserving his visions and precepts in a book or scripture.
Yet it is doubtful how much of the original fire and purpose
of the prophet persist in modern Islam. The written word,
as in Jewry, and sometimes in the Church, so easily becomes
a dead and deadening letter. Jesus left no book, and for
her first and greatest generation the Christian Church possessed no scriptures of her own.

St. Francis left behind a brotherhood of monks, a sacred
organisation of "Franciscans". But for all his care and
foresight, a generation or two sufficed to lose most of what

he wished to keep — the willing poverty, the glad humility, the gaiety of heart. Franciscans were not long recognised as true brothers-in-spirit of the greatest of the saints. Jesus left no organisation with officers, buildings, creeds, rules, and formal membership; and the existing churches sometimes seem woefully unlike that first disciple-band around the Lord.

More modern attempts to perpetuate a movement, through a society, an institution, an order or legal constitution, or a trust fund, are often lamentable failures. The fervour, the vision, the ideals, and generosity of the past cannot be caught in legal terminology and fastened upon succeeding generations. The "movement" or institution — frequently becomes a pathetic memorial, a tomb in which the spirit of the founder lies embalmed — revered but not renewed.

Clearly, this difficulty of preserving the fine impulses of the past is a real problem in the way of human progress. Yet, without formal doctrine, written Scripture, organised Church, or institution to safeguard His word and work, Jesus could still say, "It is expedient for you that I go".

II

The instance of St. Francis suggests an explanation. Francis shared with all who would consent a certain "spirit", an outlook, an infection of the soul, a purpose, and a vow. There was a true meeting and sharing of minds between the leader and the led. This method he certainly learned of Jesus; and to the extent that this method, and not organisation, was relied upon, the Franciscan movement retained its power. So Jesus, too, had left behind Him a select group of men with His impress upon their minds, His person and words within their memories, His grace within their hearts — men possessing a Christlike spirit.

Observers took knowledge of them that they had been with Jesus. They were "Christly" men, bearing in their character, outlook, attitude, and spirit the "marks" of the Lord Jesus. The place which this thought occupies in the New Testament cannot be exaggerated. The ideal of Christlikeness is everywhere: we are to be conformed to the image of God's Son, changed into the same image, grow up into the measure of the stature of the fulness of Christ, being imitators of Him and looking forward to being like Him.

The ideal describes the purpose for which we are saved, it determines the process of our discipline, it directs the movement of God's providence in our lives, it defines the Christian hope. "Let this mind be in you which was also in Christ Jesus" may be held to be the central exhortation of the Christian faith. But especially is Christlikeness emphasised where the spirit of Jesus is discussed.

"Ye know not what spirit ye are of" said Jesus to the sons of thunder, and immediately contrasted their suggestion, to call down fire upon the inhospitable Samaritans, with His own spirit, which seeks ever to save and heal and not to destroy. When Paul argues with the Corinthians about the signs of the Spirit's presence in the Church, it is to the Christlike qualities of character and life that he appeals. Where the Spirit of the Lord is, there men are changed into the same image, from glory to glory, as by the Spirit. Christ's word, "By their fruits ye shall know them" becomes in Paul's language, "if any man have not the spirit of Christ, he is none of his". The saved are like the Saviour. The Christlike spirit within the Christian is the only sure proof that the Spirit of Christ is in the life.

Such is the method Jesus relied upon for perpetuation of His work: an "apostolic succession" of men in whom, in every generation, His spirit is kindled afresh. Without such men, tradition, Scripture, organisation, and cherished memory are useless. The continuance of Christ's work depends directly upon the continuance in the earth of Christlike men.

III

But how is this to be achieved? Must not the original inspiration die away in the formalism and tradition that are the legacy of great spirits, but not their life? Would not even a given pattern of spiritual experience become stereotyped and unreal as the years passed?

The answer lies in the stupendous promise made in the upper room before Jesus went forth to die: the promise of the coming of the Spirit. All that is implied here cannot easily be summarised, nor can all that the Church has experienced of its truth be quickly told. That "God is Spirit" is an insight belonging to the highest peak of Christian revelation. That "God was in Christ" is the fundamental conviction of the Christian heart. That the same God, through Christ, by the Spirit, is now present in the ongoing life of the Church, dwelling within each Christian believer, is the very consummation of all Christ taught and did and suffered.

But this profound conception may be presented from two points of view. On the one hand, Jesus promised His disciples that in the coming years the Spirit, as the Spirit of truth, would bring to their remembrance all that He had said, would show them their way forward, would illumine their minds, and bring conviction to the world. As the Comforter, the "fortifying" Spirit, He would not leave them leaderless and vulnerable, but would equip them to confront their every foe and to endure unshaken every adverse circumstance. As the Holy Spirit, He would convince of sin, expel every desire of evil, cleanse the soul, and build up the character in Christlikeness. In the wider life of the Church men saw new things happening: fisherfolk, slaves, women, and youths testified to a divine joy, entered into a new liberty, spoke with authority, manifested unsuspected courage and endurance, and made an impact upon society quite out of proportion to their natural gifts. They had indeed "received power, after that the Holy Spirit had come upon them".

On the other hand, Jesus promised that He Himself would return. He did not intend to leave them for long. "I will come again . . . I will not leave you orphans . . . . We [the Father and I] will come and take up our abode with you . . . ." The Spirit is in some sense the substitute for Christ's physical presence: He will convey all of Christ to each suceeding generation, taking of the things of Christ and revealing them to believers. It is *almost* suggested that the risen Christ and the Holy Spirit are one: "He dwelleth with you, and shall be in you"; and Paul likewise can say: "The Lord is the Spirit", though throughout the New Testament some distinction is maintained. It was expedient that Christ should go away in death, because thus He would be liberated from the limitations of space and time, thenceforward to abide with disciples everywhere and for ever.

So those who imagined they had lost their Lord found their minds still quickened by His truth, their decisions guided by His wisdom, their steps directed by His will, their hearts encouraged, their prayers prompted, their faults rebuked, and their faith renewed, just as in His earthly presence. They discovered, with an intoxicating joy, that the *Spirit of Jesus* Himself dwelt in their hearts. Never again did these men look merely back to Jesus: they looked up. Their watchword was: "The Lord is near" — meaning, "at your elbow".

In this way the Christian faith resolves the problem of the perpetuation of Christ's cause. The work goes on because Christ lives on. In the *double* miracle of Pentecost and after, the succession of Christlike men indwelt by the Spirit of the Christ, the undying life of the Church and her renewal in each generation are ensured.

And this, too, is part of the story of Jesus: for the story has no end. All that happened long ago in Galilee and Jerusalem is extended down through history to the present day. The Spirit of truth keeps the Christian mind free from mere tradition and dead rules; the Spirit of life and power keeps the Christian outlook hopeful, free, and forward-looking; the Spirit of holiness perpetually reforms and cleanses the Church of Christ amidst a sinful world. Christ in us is the only hope of long continuance and final glory. As Peter said at Pentecost, "the promise is to you, and to your children, and to all that are afar off . . .".

That includes the twentieth century — and onwards, "till he come".

35 The Coming King

"This same Jesus . . . shall so come . . . ."
"When the Son of man cometh, shall he find faith on the earth?"
"Till he come."

Acts 1:11, Luke 18:8, I Corinthians 11:26

FOR SIXTEEN HUNDRED years the Christian Church has sung in the glorious poetry of the *Te Deum*, "We believe that Thou shalt come to be our Judge". For still longer she has confessed in the Apostles' Creed, "He shall come to judge the quick and the dead". Before either anthem or creed, the New Testament had crystallised the glowing apostolic hope: "This same Jesus shall so come . . . . The Lord himself shall descend from heaven . . . . Christ, who is our life, shall appear . . . . We wait for his Son from heaven . . unto the coming of the Lord Jesus . . . . When he shall appear, we shall be like him."

Earlier yet, even before the New Testament was written, the Church gathered regularly on the first day of the week around the Lord's table to "show the Lord's death till he come". And often in her worship, her correspondence, and her friendly greetings occurred the very ancient phrase, untranslated from the Aramaic mother-tongue of Christianity, "Maranatha" — "Lord, come!" So in her praise, her confession of faith, her Scriptures and her worship, the Church from the beginning has treasured the hope that Jesus somehow, some day, will return.

I

It is well to remember this constant witness to the Advent faith. By some curious misunderstanding, the doctrine of Christ's "coming" has sometimes been regarded as a "new" truth, or one recently recovered from long obscurity. With so much to remind her, the Church could scarcely forget her hope; nor could she mistake the clear words of Jesus. "The Son of man cometh on the clouds of heaven . . . .

Watch, for ye know not the day nor the hour when the Son of man cometh . . . . Be ye like men that wait for their Lord." Again and again, in the parables of judgement and of service, the idea is reiterated: an absent Lord, an arriving Bridegroom, a task to be pursued until the lord of the servants returns. In all such sayings, however much may be due to oriental imagery and emphasis, the central truth is inescapable: Christ will come again. "Blessed are those servants whom the lord when he cometh shall find watching: be ye therefore ready, for the Son of man cometh at an hour when ye think not."

Without cavalier denial of her Lord, the Church could scarcely doubt promises so clear or ignore warnings so urgent.

II

But if the hope of Christ's appearing has never been lost, it has often been discredited. Some misguided zealots have pretended to know more than has been revealed about the coming of Christ. Jesus confessed that "of that day and hour knoweth no man, neither the Son, but the Father", and in His parting words He admonished the disciples: "It is not for you to know the times or the seasons which the Father hath put in his own power". Throughout the Gospels, it is precisely ignorance of the set time and programme of events which lends cogency to the repeated exhortations to be ready. Only an impious conceit can pretend to know what Jesus declared to be God's secret.

The Advent hope is discredited similarly by those who so dwell upon the wonder, the glory, the spectacular marvels they claim to foresee "at the end of the world" as to over-shadow the equally wonderful and still more precious truth that Christ is with us always. Both things are essential elements of Christian faith: He is beside us already, He is coming in glory. The hope of His *coming* must never obscure the truth of His equally wonderful, equally glorious, *companionship*.

A third way by which the Advent faith has been for many made repellent is by its association with horrifying forecasts of an Advent doom, with threats of divine terror and super-natural violence, and with misquoted phrases like "with the breath of his mouth he shall slay the wicked", and "in flaming fire taking vengeance". Sub-Christian imagination playing around the unquestionable truth of final judgement has served to distort the central emphasis of the New Testament hope, that *this same Jesus shall so come*".

We cannot be reminded too often that He who comes is not some dreadful Christ conjured up by vengeful imagination or barely concealed "spiritual spitefulness", but the same Jesus who lay in beauty at Bethlehem, who taught gracious truth in glowing words at Nazareth, who healed and befriended the poor in Galilee, who took a child upon His knee, and who set the crowds laughing at the grotesque excesses of Pharisaism.

He will be the same Jesus who looked with love at erring Peter, rode humbly into Jerusalem on a donkey, girded Himself with a towel to wash the disciples' feet, and bore at Calvary in sorrow and agony the sins of the world. If we cannot see power and majesty and glory *in such guise*, then we have not yet learned to think His thoughts and judge by His standards what power and majesty and glory mean.

Jesus comes again; to victory, but it is the victory of love; to judgement, but it is still the judgement of truth and not of violence; to accomplish the consummation of the age, but it is the age of the gospel; in glory, and His glory, as before, will be full of grace and truth. We wait for this same Jesus.

III

The hope of Christ's return is not just a happy ending to a heart-rending story. Nor is it mere curiosity about the future inventing its own solutions. Without this forward dimension of Christian faith our assessment of Jesus would be incomplete. Without some form of Advent hope, His Lordship over history remains only an abstract idea, lacking significance or confirmation. Without the Advent expectation, the long story of Christ's suffering and death would lack its ultimate moral vindication — not in reprisal or revenge, but in fulfilment. Without an Advent goal, the course of history seems a dreary vista of endless cycles of sin, suffering, and sorrow eternally repeated in a meaningless dance of phantoms.

For the Christian can cling to no vain illusion of inevitable progress through the ingenuity or the perfectibility of unaided man: he knows man too well. In place of the fashionable extremes — the sceptic pessimism of a purposeless universe, and the shallow optimism of a humanist assumption unsupported by experience — the Christian believes that the long story of mankind, with Christ within it, will rise at last to a great Day of the Lord, when the purposes of God shall be complete, when the earth shall be filled with the knowledge of God as the waters cover the sea, when Christ shall reign and God shall be all in all.

> *Surely He cometh, and a thousand voices*
> *Shout to the saints, and to the deaf are dumb:*
> *Surely He cometh, and the earth rejoices,*
> *Glad in His coming, Who hath sworn, "I come".*

Yet it is not comfort only that the hope of Christ's appearing quickens in Christian hearts, but an abiding moral inspiration. In the parables of the talents, the pounds, the faithless steward, and the watchful servants, the Advent hope is closely linked to consecrated service: the servant must be ready to give account of his stewardship. "Watch ye therefore and pray always that ye may be accounted worthy to stand before the Son of man." Equally, the Advent hope is related to Christlike living: "Knowing the time . . . the night is far spent, the day is at hand, let us cast off the works of darkness and put on the armour of light; let us walk honestly, as in the day . . . . We know that when he shall appear we shall be like him; and every man that hath this hope in him purifieth himself". This is the crown laid up for "all them that love His appearing".

IV

Problems and questions abound when imagination seeks to pierce the future and picture for itself the end of history. This is no less true of secular, sceptical, or scientific thought than of Christian faith. The wise and instructed Christian humbly confesses ignorance about method, programme, and form:

I cannot tell how all the lands shall worship,
  When, at His bidding, every storm is stilled,
Or who can say how great the jubilation
  When all the hearts of men with love are filled.
But this I know, the skies will thrill with rapture,
  And myriad, myriad human voices sing,
And earth to heaven, and heaven to earth, will answer
  At last the Saviour, Saviour of the world, is King!

For the Christian knows that his life is poised between two divine interventions into history, anchored as it were in the seas of time by the twin chains of memory and hope. He looks back to see divine love working out redemption through suffering and death; he looks forward to see that same love working out victory through judgement and glory. Thus made vividly aware of the eternal issues bound up with the story of Jesus, the Christian knows with unshakable inner certainty that the crucial, final question is not our assessment of the Stranger of Galilee, but His assessment of ourselves. He knows that what ultimately matters for every soul is not whether we shall have to say, "Who art thou, Lord?" but whether, in sad finality Christ will have to say, "Depart from me, *I never knew you!*"

ENVOY

CHRIST IN THE UNIVERSE

With this ambiguous earth
His dealings have been told us. These abide:
The signal to a maid, the human birth,
The lesson, and the young Man crucified.

But not a star of all
The innumerable host of stars has heard
How He administered this terrestrial ball.
Our race have kept their Lord's entrusted Word.

Of His earth-visiting feet
None knows the secret, cherished, perilous,
The terrible, shamefast, frightened, whispered, sweet,
Heart-shattering secret of His way with us.

No planet knows that this
Our wayside planet, carrying land and wave,
Love and life multiplied, and pain and bliss,
Bears, as chief treasure, one forsaken grave.

Nor, in our little day,
May His devices with the heavens be guessed,
His pilgrimage to thread the Milky Way
Or His bestowals there be manifest.

But in the eternities,
Doubtless we shall compare together, hear
A million alien Gospels, in what guise
He trod the Pleiades, the Lyre, the Bear.

O, be prepared, my soul!
To read the inconceivable, to scan
The million forms of God those stars unroll
When, in our turn, we show to them a Man.

ALICE MEYNELL